# Discover paradise

A selection of stories from Air Niugini's in-flight magazine - Paradise

Edited by Geoff McLaughlin MBE

# Contributors

Greg Bluett

Keith Briggs

Dean Butler

Nancy Cohen

Jean-Michael Cousteau

David Eastburn

Tim Flannery

Jean Paul Ferrero

Michael Gebicki

Kevin Glennon

Keith Graham

Bob Halstead

Rani Hesketh

Bruce Hoy

Tony Karacsonyi

Atairo Kanisuwo

Lyn & Pat Manly

R.C. Murphy

Pamela C. Rosi

Peter Schouten

Greg Smith

Peter Stone

Ingrid & Oliver Strewe

Liz Thompson

Grant Trewenack

Air Niugini in its promotion of the country has used the slogan "Papua New Guinea, Land Of The Unexpected", "Like No Place You've Ever Been." Since 1976 an enormous variety of articles published in each issue of Air Niugini inflight magazine, "Paradise", has proven that this slogan in reality is fact.

This has not been planned nor were the articles for each Paradise edition selected to portray this impression, articles were selected for publication on their own merits.

In this issue of *"Discover Paradise"* we included a selection of articles from various issues of Paradise magazines, you are provided with an insight into the numerous cultures of Papua New Guinea, a Highlands Compensation Ceremony, a display of Sepik River Carvings, the history of the Asaro Mudman and the making of the Kundu Drum.

"Discover Paradise" also features articles from a range of wonderful dive sites, in clear, warm water diving on wrecks or amongst coral, swimming with sharks or finding Golden Cowrie shells, in our divers paradise.

I trust that you enjoy our limited coverage of this great country.

**DIETER SEEFELD**
Chief Executive
Air Niugini

Published by
Geoff McLaughlin MBE
P.O. Box 7186, Boroko,
Papua New Guinea,
for Air Niugini,
the National Airline
of Papua New Guinea
Air Niugini House, Jacksons Airport,
Port Moresby
Phone: 273 415  Fax: 273 416

® Copyright Air Niugini 1992

Editor: Geoff McLaughlin MBE
ISBN No: 9980-907-924
All Rights reserved

Printed by Progressive Printing Agency
Hong Kong
Ph: 563 0145  Fax: 811 1344

DISTRIBUTOR:

La Galamo Books
P.O. Box 1405
Lae-Morobe Province
Tel/Fax: (675) 42 2588

# Contents

**Above** *Resin is easily removed with help of ubiquitous bushknife.*

**Left** *Resin seeping from a bark cut.* **above** *Fresh resin is soft.*

Fire to cook food and provide light has been essential since the human race began. Various combustible materials can be used to provide light but most of them flare briefly and are not very controllable. The only traditional product to combine ready availability, portability and a steady, long lasting flame is the resin torch.

Several tree species in the Papua New Guinea bush exude a thick resinous sap when the bark is cut or bruised. Colors of the resin can be frosty white, honey brown or almost black.

TUMBU

Once dry, this resin is quite flammable and is the fuel of 'tumbuna lait', traditional light.

Villagers regularly cut the bark of resin-producing trees with a bush knife or axe to maintain a continuing supply. It is usually left to dry there on the bark in blobs or stalactites which are later prised off. If some of the resin is still slightly pliable when gathered, it will be left in a container on a rack above a cooking fire until it is dry and rather brittle.

A person making a resin torch places a smooth stone in a bark basin and, laying each piece of resin on the stone, pounds and crushes it to a coarse powder of crystalline granules.

The torch maker has on hand long narrow leaves that have been softened by heating over the fire so they can be formed into a hollow trough-like shape which they retain when cooled. Laying two or three thicknesses of these leaves together to form a canoe like receptacle the torch maker empties the crushed resin into it, ensuring it is evenly spread along its length. The top leaves are closed over to completely encase the granules and a few turns of fine string-like creeper around the parcel hold it together.

The binding is made by stripping the skin off a soft creeper. This is wound tightly around the torch and pulled firm by a series of half-hitch knots along its length. The finished torch is stuck into the under side of the roof thatch above the fire where it dries out completely. It usually stays there, safe and dry until needed.

The resin torch lights readily when poked into the glowing coals of a fire. Once alight it is propped up in a convenient spot in the centre of the main living room. As it burns, a black char forms around the rim at the top. This will grow toward the centre of the burning pool of molten resin, effectively sealing it off and extinguishing the

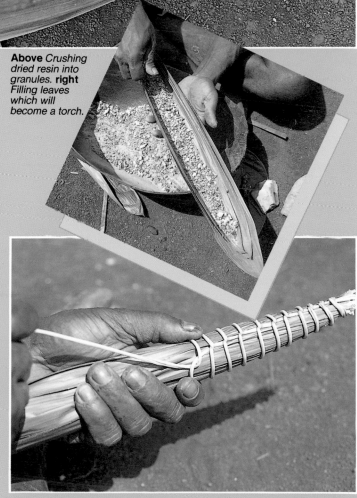

**Above** Crushing dried resin into granules. **right** Filling leaves which will become a torch.

**Above** Soft cane binds the leaves full of resin.

Story and Photographs by Keith Briggs

A LAIT

**Above** *Torches suspended to dry.*

**Right** *Enough light for reading.*

flame. To prevent this, there is always someone close by to scrape the char off with a small stick, chip or splinter of firewood, keeping it burning brightly.

The lighted torch gives off a pleasant resinous smell and a thin pencil of black smoke. When men are decorating their bodies for a singsing, they hold the concave side of a piece of newly-cut banana stalk above and close to the flame, on which it deposits a layer of rich, black soot. Wiped off with the finger and mixed with tree oil, the soot becomes the shiny black paint so often seen on the skin of Papua New Guinean traditional dancers.

People travelling through the bush at night use leaves to form a hood around the flame so their movement does not douse the light. When spearing prawns or yabbies at night, the hunter binds or holds a large shiny leaf around the top of the torch in the shape of a reflector to concentrate the light, enabling him to more effectively spot the tell-tale reflection from the crustaceans' eyes. This also shields the hunter's eyes from the glare. enabling him to retain his night vision beyond the torch.

In most village houses one can find the remains of an old kerosene lamp, with tank rusted out, the glass or some mechanical part broken or missing. Near the fireplace there will very likely be a spot that held the end of a cigar-shaped torch and a flat stone with shiny black blobs on it where the burning resin dripped. Lamps will come and go, kerosene may be hard to get in the bush or be too expensive to buy, but there will always be the resin trees, the leaves and the binding vines. Likewise, in the most palatial homes in any city where hydro, coal or even nuclear power generates electricity for lighting, one will find tallow candles in the cupboards.

**Below** *Dinner by tumbuna lait.* **inset** *A torch ready for use.*

**Left** *Unloading supplies from a Junkers W34 on Lake Kutubu.*
**bottom left** *Lake Kutubu, discovered by aerial survey in 1936.*
**above** *Tari Basin from air.*

# CORRUGATED
## *Kites*

Story and photography by David Eastburn

No country owes as much to the aeroplane for its development as Papua New Guinea. This is despite a statement made in the early 1920s by the famous aviator, Sir Charles Kingsford-Smith, that New Guinea was no place for aeroplanes!

PNG's first commercial aeroplane, a tiny de Havilland DH37 biplane, began operating between Lae and Wau on the Morobe goldfields in April, 1927. By the end of the decade, the Mandated Territory of New Guinea, as the northern half of PNG was then known, was a world leader in civil aviation. It maintained that status throughout the 1930s.

Leadership in civil aviation was due to the vision and daring of a few remarkable men who were able to see the potential of aeroplanes as cargo carriers in this rugged land. It was made possible by a remarkable family of metal aircraft, the Junkers.

Junkers produced the most advanced and largest commercial cargo transport aircraft in the world in the 1920s. The trademark of Junkers aeroplanes was their corrugated aluminium skinning, which gave them the appearance of being constructed of roofing iron, but was the source of their great strength and durability. These aircraft captured many world airfreight records

for the Mandated Territory as they transported supplies and materials, including the components of eight huge dredges, into the Morobe goldfields, during the late 1920s and the 1930s.

The first to recognise the potential value of aircraft as cargo carriers in PNG was Cecil Levien, a former kiap (patrol officer) turned miner. He saw that the system of using carriers to transport food and supplies from the coast over the mountains to the Morobe goldfields was both inefficient and cruel.

After the Edie Creek rush in 1926, Levien persuaded his backers, Guinea Gold No Liability, to purchase an aeroplane to supply the goldfields. The aircraft was a success and others soon followed. However, these were wood, wire and fabric biplanes unsuited to tropical conditions and of designs little changed since World War I.

'Pard' Mustar, who had been employed to fly the Guinea Gold DH37, made Levien aware of the German Junkers W34, an advanced, all metal, single-engined freighter aircraft. The W34 would be ideal for the type of work on the goldfields and its metal construction would not be affected by the tropical conditions. Mustar, with strong support from Levien, was able to convince Guinea Gold to buy this expensive aeroplane. Guinea Gold then formed a new company to operate its aircraft, Guinea Airways Limited.

Mustar went to Germany to test fly and purchase a Junkers W34. He found its performance, carrying capacity and ease of loading to be even better than expected. The new aeroplane was shipped from Hamburg and arrived in Rabaul in March, 1928. It was registered VH-UGZ and was later known as Guinea Airways No. 1 Junkers.

On its first flight from Lae to Wau, in April, VH-UGZ carried one passenger and a tonne of freight. The amount of cargo transported in this 40-minute flight would have taken 100 carriers eight days. In its first 19 days of flying, VH-UGZ earned Guinea Airways the equivalent of K57,000 net, in today's values.

By the end of the year it had carried around 500 passengers and 300 tonnes of freight. So successful was the first W34 that others were soon ordered.

Due mainly to VH-UGZ, more tonnage was airfreighted in the Mandated Territory of New Guinea, in 1928, than by all Australian airlines combined. This was the first of many freight records which would fall to New Guinea and Junkers aircraft over the next decade.

The surface gold on the Morobe goldfields was soon exhausted, but vast quantities remained, mixed with the alluvium and gravels in the Bulolo Valley. It could be profitably extracted only by dredges which could quickly and efficiently treat millions of tonnes of earth. Placer Development Limited was interested in dredging. However, the terrain between the coast and the goldfields was too rugged to build a road easily and dredging equipment was too large and heavy to be transported in any other way.

The managing director of Placer, Charles Banks, made the ingenious suggestion that dredges could be designed so that they could be airfreighted in pieces to the goldfields and assembled on site. However, it

**Left** Junkers W34 near Mt Hagen in 1933. **centre** Lake Kutubu at dawn. **above right** Unloading Junkers G31 at Wau. **below right** Cricket tournament players at Salamaua in 1933 with their transport, a Junkers W34.

Left *Part of a huge gold dredge airlifted to Bulolo.*
above *Lae Aerodrome, 1931, with three G31s and two W34s.*

was found that the tumbler shaft, the drive shaft of a dredge, could not be made lighter than 3.5 tonnes, much too heavy for the available aircraft to lift.

'Pard' Mustar, who was responsible for the introduction of the first Junkers aeroplanes, was again to influence the history of PNG aviation. He told Charles Banks about the giant G31 tri-motor aircraft being developed by Junkers. Mustar learned of this aircraft while in Germany collecting the first W34. The G31 was capable of lifting the heaviest part of a dredge and the bulkiest pieces could be

easily loaded through a large roof hatch.

Banks convinced his fellow directors to take up the mining leases in the Bulolo Valley. Placer formed an operating Company, Bulolo Gold Dredging Limited (BGD) and arranged for the purchase of two Junkers G31s. BGD arranged with Guinea Airways to operate and maintain their aircraft. Guinea Airways also bought a G31, and BGD later added a third to its fleet. The success of this daring operation depended entirely on air transport and specifically on the Junkers G31s.

What followed was the grea-

test achievement in PNG aviation, the famous airlift of dredges into the Morobe goldfields. Between March, 1931 and November, 1939, the historic airlift transported the components of eight dredges, hydro-electricity plants, workshops, machinery and houses, from the coast to the goldfields. Two of the dredges weighed almost 4,000 tonnes each and were, at the time, the largest in the world. The first dredge went into service in March, 1932 and the eighth was in operation by November, 1939.

World airfreight records were constantly broken. During one month in 1931, the Junkers aircraft operated by Guinea Airways carried more freight than any other airline in the world for the whole year!

This romantic era in PNG aviation ended abruptly, in a hail of Japanese bullets.

On January 21, 1942, Japanese aircraft attacked Lae, Salamaua and Bulolo, destroying most of the civilian air fleet.

Corrugated tri-motors appeared briefly in the skies over Papua New Guinea again after World War II. Gibbes Sepik Airways bought three Junkers Ju 52/3ms, similar to those flown by the Luftwaffe as troop and freight carriers during World War II. These aircraft were successfully used to service Highland stations for a short time in the late 1950s.

# Mary Gole

Story and photographs by Liz Thompson

**Right** *A storage jar in the unique pottery style of Mary Gole (inset).*

Large, fat, rounded coil pots sit on the shelves of Mary Gole's small, home studio. Shiny brown surfaces into which black linear designs are cut; strange, animal-like patterns evoking a sense of ancient stories and fireside legends. Gole is one of Papua New Guinea's many professional potters and one of the most renowned.

A wonderfully, warm-spirited woman, she works from her studio attached to the side of her Port Moresby home. Her face is decorated with tattoos which are mirrored in the designs on some of her pots. Her hands move from water to clay, gently moulding, twisting, building the beautiful pots and objects which decorate most of the available space around her. Gole has her own style which sits unique among her contemporaries.

The round pots are particularly beautiful; full, satisfying shapes which invite hands to run across the surface. Using a traditional building method of clay coils, Gole draws on traditional designs and ideas but with a considerable amount of improvisation. She has adapted the clay she uses, working with the locally found material and mixing it with other stronger more durable forms in order that her work can travel. This allows her to exhibit overseas and encourages foreign buyers.

**Top** *Mary Gole in her studio.* **below** *Distinctive Mary Gole storage jar.* **centre** *Instruments of the potter's art.* **upper right** *Decorated clay fruits.* **lower right** *Grass to be used to weave string bags (bilums).*

Her mother was a potter but Gole did not immediately make it a family tradition. Married and with children she considers herself to have been a housewife until relatively late in life. By making pots she began a personal course of creative experimentation.

She wears a cotton dress, hand-printed fabric, one of her own designs. On the walls of the house hang bilums she has woven from twisted strands of bark, dyed with the colored residue of boiled leaves. On the shelves, the floor and tables sit pots of all shapes and sizes. Large, water-cooling pots with lids and handles in the shapes of animals. Small cooking pots, long thin clay containers which hold brushes and branches of dried leaves. Broad oval bowls, small round dishes. There are pots with faces etched into their sides, noses and eyebrows which stand out in relief, pots with designs cut deep into their surfaces. Around and alongside all this hang gourds, shells, dried seed pods, pieces of nature which have provided inspiration. Small pieces of dried leaves, round weathered stones, the suggestion of their shapes and patterns subtly being translated into her work.

All the clay work is bisked in a kiln then fired with seaweed, cooking salt and sawdust which leaves a stunning earth colored finish. As the salt melts on the pots it coats and makes them stronger. After firing they are rubbed with coconut oil which gives them a rich, shiny surface. Gole rarely glazes her work, disliking the artificial sense of color, finding it too bright. Only occasionally, on delicate clay necklaces and wind charms will she compromise and use a clear glaze.

While strongly original, the work clearly draws on traditional influences, from her village and from designs and shapes of pottery produced throughout PNG. Margaret Tuxton's book on PNG potters, which illustrates work from throughout the country, is something she often draws from and uses as a source of inspiration. Though her mother made larger pots, invariably plain, with no designs, Gole's work is the opposite. Linear traces draw the stories of animals and legends, of women at work, of day-to-day events, images relating anything in which she finds interest. Strange new developments and the beginnings of new ideas, some to be further explored, some abandoned, lie along the shelves.

**Top** *A well-used Mary Gole clay pot oven.* **far left & left** *Bowls by the artist.* **above** *Tools of the trade.*

Clay eggplants, clay fruits etched with small circular designs, small clay figures in a variety of positions, many wild and wonderful things. But she draws the line, she insists, at dinner sets, despite having been asked to make them on many occasions.

Involved in the PNG potter society, she also teaches children how to work with clay. At the Waigani Art Centre and the East Boroko School, she teaches children aged from 6 to 14 how to build traditional hand-made pots. Annually exhibiting at the Waigani Arts and Crafts Exhibition, she represented PNG as a potter at the 1988 South Pacific Arts Festival in Townsville, Australia. Along with other potters from the Eastern Highlands Cultural Centre she sold work and demonstrated the kinds of techniques she uses. Several years ago she visited Bangladesh along with 177 other artists for a similar purpose, to show her work and participate in workshops for 10 days.

While most of the work is utilitarian, it is extremely attractive in its own right. Mary Gole is yet another example of PNG's numerous and extremely talented, contemporary artists, who, while producing work based on traditional methods, draw from modern day influences and the diversity of inspiration PNG has to offer.

**Top** *Kiln stacked for firing.* **far left** *Coil pot with snake motif.* **upper centre** *Mary Gole with her bilums (string bags).* **lower centre** *Bowl with elaborate decoration.* **above** *Small jar.*

**Story and photographs by Keith Briggs**

# Kundu

**Left & inset** *Kaluli dancers play and tune their kundu drums.*

A round the world, certain crafts seem to be concentrated in a given place. The Black Forest area in Germany is known for its clockmakers and the glassblowers of Venice have become world famous. Some villages in Papua New Guinea are known for the dogs they breed, the stone clubs they make or other small distinctions. In the Southern Highlands Province, the men of Wasu Village have achieved fame as the most prolific drum-makers in their language group.

The kundu drum can be found throughout the country and is perhaps the universal musical instrument of PNG. It comes in many shapes and sizes, from short and stumpy specimens to those more than 1.5 metres long, found around the Nomad River in the Western Province.

Whenever I see PNG craftsmanship I wonder how these things were made before the introduction of steel tools. The answer is always a fascinating revelation of ingenuity and the clever use of natural materials.

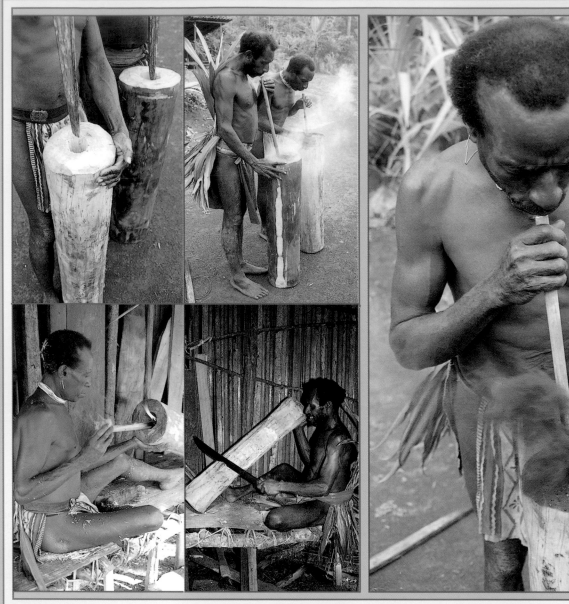

**Top left & right** *Hollowing out drum blanks.* **below left** *Burning out the centre.* **below right** *Carving the outer shape.*

**Above** *Using a blow pipe to purge powdered charcoal and ash.*

Only a few trees are suitable for producing the blanks for making kundu drums. Traditionally, sharpened crowbar-like pieces of black palm were used to gouge a depression in the heart wood at the end of the upstanding blank. Glowing charcoal from a hard bark was crumbled into this pocket and then air blown onto it using a bamboo tube until the fire glowed and roared like a miniature furnace. A good supply of tubes was kept on hand as the heat soon consumed them. The drum-maker carefully guided the glowing mass until the centre was burned out parallel with the outside. The hole was tapered, with the outer ends being wider than the centre. When ash and spent charcoal blocked the inside working area, the drum maker used a black palm bar to pound the debris. The resulting powder was blown out with a bamboo tube. The process was repeated until the hole was half-way through; the blank was then turned over and the operation continued until the holes met in the centre.

Nowadays bush knives with extended black palm handles are used to carve the char out of the tube. A blazing bamboo torch is passed through to burn any splinters and irregularities, then the inside is smoothed with the long knife. The outside of the instrument is finished using a normal bush knife.

As soon as the outer shape is formed, the maker closes the

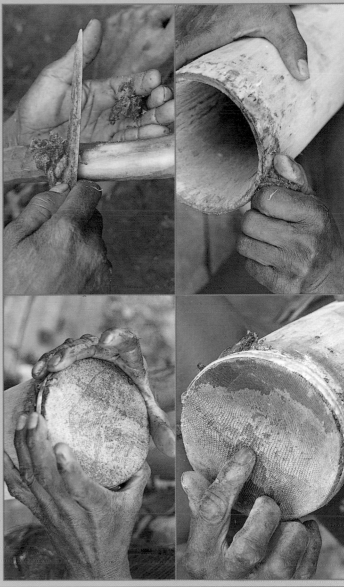

**Above** *Lizard skin is removed from storage in ash.*

**Top left & right** *Preparing and applying natural glue.* **bottom left & right** *Fitting lizard skin and removing scales.*

unfinished drum with lizard or snake skin to discover whether it will 'speak' well before he puts any more time or energy into it. Those that will not speak well are discarded and the skin kept for future use.

Lizards are hunted at night when they lie along the top of tree limbs to avoid detection. The skin is carefully removed and resembles a garment with four short sleeves. As the drum head uses the belly area, the skin is slit along the centre back. It is folded and kept in a bamboo tube compacted in ash with the ends sealed, to prevent cockroaches eating holes in it. Removed from the tube the skin is dusted off then soaked in water for softening.

Natural glue is used to attach the skin to the drum, made when the bark of a thick vine is pared down to the sappy underbark. A wad of this sticky fibrous extract is squeezed and the exuded glue then smeared around the mouth of the drum. The skin is stretched over the mouth and, precisely fitting cane bands are drawn over to hold the skin securely. Any wrinkles are smoothed by pulling at the circumference of the skin while the glue is still elastic. The glue is dried by holding the drum head over a low fire or subjecting it to heat from a bamboo torch.

Once the glue has set, all scales are carefully scraped off with a fingernail to ensure the knobs of beeswax adhere properly. Small pellets of beeswax are rolled and stuck

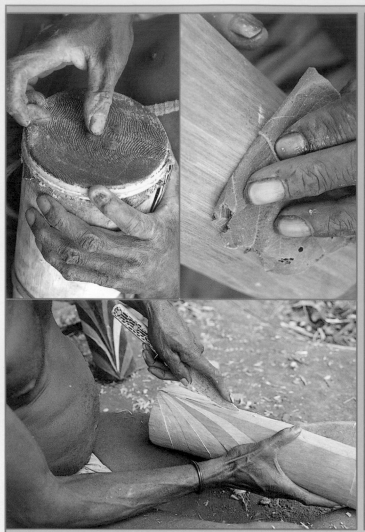

**Top left** *Sticking on beeswax for tuning.* **top right** *Smoothing with 'sandpaper' leaves.* **bottom** *Carving designs on finished drum.*

onto the skin. The drum is now roughly tuned by changing the shape or position of the beeswax and by huffing on the skin to warm it. If it promises to speak with a clear ringing voice the maker is satisfied and begins to carve the pattern on the outside. Traditionally this was done with a piece of flinty stone split to form a fine sharp edge. It is now achieved with a small steel knife. 'Sandpaper' leaves are used to give the whole job a smooth finish.

The drum is now decorated with natural dyes. Traditionally, red coloring was prepared by grinding a soft stone and mixing it with water. Today seeds from an introduced tree are preferred because of their convenience and vivid color. The tree pods are split and the seeds mixed with a little water to release the bright red dye which is applied using a brush

made by chewing or pounding the end of a flat sliver of stick.

Light coloring is created from a special clay, which dries to a light blue grey. Black paint is obtained by taking thin slices off the bark of a unique tree, causing the dark sap to ooze from the wounds. This sap causes large painful sores if it touches soft skin. Although applied by a tough calloused finger, the painter washes his hands as soon as the job is done. The sap turns new pink or white wood to a rich brown which, after 20 minutes or so, becomes quite black.

A sling or strap is woven of natural fibre and fitted to enable the drummer to grip the drum tightly. The kundu is then ready to entertain and stir the emotions with its distinctive booming note.

**Top left** *Red dye seeds.* **top right & bottom** *Putting on the finishing touches.*

• Wasu

**Above** *Typical village accommodation in the Tufi region.*

# FIORDLAND PNG

**Below** *Tufi fiord.*

**Story and photographs by Greg Smith**

"Hello. My name is Carson from Kofure village. Are you Mr Greg Smith?" So it was that my wife and I began a memorable few days as guests of Kofure village at Tufi. Many potential tourists choose not to come to Papua New Guinea because of the mass of unfavorable publicity and a general lack of media balance.

Be assured that there are places to go, people to see and things to do in the Land Of The Unexpected that are in stark contrast to the familiar press reports.

Oro Province (it may be Northern on your map) has so far missed the boom of gold, copper and oil which herald great changes in much of the mainland and in the island provinces. But it does have Tufi, the spectacular point at the northern end of Collingwood Bay, where the fiords of Scandinavia and south-west New Zealand have been transplanted into a brilliant tropical setting.

Tufi is a village of several hundred people with a government station, fish packaging plant, hotel, trade stores, school and airstrip. There are many smaller villages in the surrounding area, some built right at the water's edge while others sit high up on narrow ridge tops overlooking the sea.

Most building is done with traditional bush materials, though there is the occasional piece of corrugated iron or plastic sheeting. At locations each side of Tufi there is village accommodation available at a daily rate of around K20 all inclusive. Most have beaches and easy access to the coral reefs but lack such 'essentials' as telephone, electricity, television, noisy neighbors and motor vehicles.

Thirty minutes by light aircraft from Popondetta's Girua airport and the plane circles over the true paradise as it gently glides in across the flat, blue-green sea to touch down on the rich green of Tufi's grass strip. By prior arrangement from Port Moresby or Popondetta, someone from your chosen village guest house will greet you warmly, grab your luggage and invite you to follow. Then it's on to a platform between the waiting canoe and its single outrigger while the craft is deftly paddled and poled over and through the coral to your destination.

Upon our arrival at Kofure we were met and welcomed by a contingent of adults, teenagers and children all eager to carry our gear and show us to our temporary home. Built of bush material, it was complete with verandah and furnished with two chairs, a table, foam mattresses and mosquito nets. Who could wish for more?

Service to the guests at Kofure is typical of village life, where everyone contributes in some way, by providing garden produce, fishing, carrying water or preparing meals. And what meals! Despite very basic facilities, Vivian, the delightful young girl in charge of the kitchen, produced meals fit for royalty. Fish, poultry, mountains of vegetables, lobster, bananas, pineapple, pawpaw, watermelon and coconut filled the table three times a day. If there is a better way to enjoy a meal than sitting among the coconut palms while gazing over the brilliant blue of the sea as outrigger canoes slice serenely through the water, then someone has been hiding it from me all these years.

**Left** *Kofure Village beach.* **below** *Guest transfer, Tufi-style.*

Days at Kofure can be as relaxing or as energetic as the guest requires. After greeting the sunrise of the new day while enjoying tea or coffee there is swimming from the white, sandy beach only 50 metres away. This can be combined with snorkelling to marvel at the infinite variety of coral and other marine life. Humans are not the only animals that find the waters off Tufi hold a great charm.

After an overwhelming breakfast, there can be more of the same, or a time to laze, or an interesting discussion of history and tradition. While the hosts never intrude, they are always at hand to talk or to offer advice.

Typical of the no-cost extras that are provided was a two-hour canoe trip with Sore, an ex-teacher who has returned to his Kofure roots. Between snorkelling stops he entertained us with stories of his people and their legends; legends which have so much more impact when spoken than when written.

**Centre, below** *Tufi family group in their bilas (finery).* **bottom** *Coming home through the shallows after a day at market.*

For the cost of the fuel it was arranged for a member of the village to take us the full length of the Tufi fiord in his outboard powered aluminium dinghy. As the fiord narrowed we entered a different world, a world enclosed by thick mangroves, massive pandanus palms and sago palms and watched over by towering, vertical cliffs.

We tethered the dinghy, now above the tidal reaches, in clear mountain water to walk through and marvel at the forest. Only 200 metres on we struck an unexpected bonus; Sore's uncle and his family were making sago. A son was cutting the pulp from a newly felled palm which was then carried by a daughter (home on leave from her office job in Port Moresby) to her father who had the task of squeezing the sago from the pulp to let it settle in the trough before the final processing and transporting back to their village many kilometres away. They were thrilled that we were so interested in their tradition and took great trouble to explain the details of the operation.

Two things stand out to the visitor as special cultural aspects of the Tufi area. The first is tapa cloth made by many hours of pounding the bark of a special tree and further hours of meticulous painting of the designs in black (charcoal) and red (boiled bark). The tapa is worn by both male and female at traditional gatherings and the purchase of a length makes not only a great wallhanging but a constant reminder of the Tufi experience.

The second aspect is the intricate facial tattoos of many of the women and late teenage girls. Applied by pricking the skin with a sharp thorn and rubbing dye into the punctures, these tattoos are living, breathing works of art. Admiring these designs seems to put their owners at ease and they are usually happy to explain the process and the not inconsiderable pain involved.

To discuss both traditional ways and the merits of the world's leaders, to have small children who speak no English readily agreeing to pose for the camera, to find a beautiful girl with tattooed face and a Westpac T-shirt is to realise that people are more alike than different despite their color and culture.

To walk unguarded and without fear along Kofure's white sand in the moonlight is to give a large thumbs down to a common perception of PNG.

Top *Tufi villager dressed for a singsing.* far right *Palm forest provides food (sago) and transport (canoe logs).* right *Fresh fish for dinner.*

Above left *'The Huli'* *1986, acrylic by Larry Santana.* **above right** *The artist on East 44th Street, Manhattan.*

Story and photographs
by Pamela C. Rosi

On a cold, winter morning at Newark Airport, New Jersey, USA, my husband and I greeted a young contemporary artist from Papua New Guinea, Larry Santana. Three years earlier, I first met Larry at the National Arts School in Port Moresby, where I was doing research on contemporary PNG art. He invited me to his house and for several months I returned often to discuss his painting and life as an artist.

# Larry Santana

**This page** *Larry Santana at New York's Rockefeller Center; on the steps of the New York Metropolitan Museum; and painting at a Life Drawing class, Bridgewater College.*

When I left PNG, we were good friends and I thought it would be some time before we would meet again.

Thanks, however, to the sponsorship of his employer, Larry was coming to the United States to attend the opening of an exhibition of contemporary Papua New Guinean art which I was curating at Bridgewater State College, Massachusetts. We were to be guests at the college for three days, giving Larry a special opportunity to speak about his art to Americans and to tell them something about PNG. I hoped that during his visit Larry would learn something interesting about Americans.

Suddenly, there was Larry walking towards us dressed in a warm winter jacket against the cold. He saw us, smiled broadly, and we embraced. Larry's two-week adventure in the United States had begun.

Monmouth Beach, our home, is a small seaside community where life is typically quiet and uneventful. It is, however, within commuting distance of New York so, before going to Bridgewater, my plan was to introduce Larry to the culture and colorful sights of life in the 'Big Apple'.

The morning after Larry's arrival, we took a train ride — Larry's first — bound for Pennsylvania Station in midtown Manhattan. As always, the place was packed and we waited in line half an hour to get a taxi. Then caught in the midday gridlock, our taxi barely moved and the driver, together with thousands of others, vented his frustration by continually honking his horn.

The unaccustomed noise was nerve-wracking for Larry but, as we moved uptown, he was able to catch a glimpse of some of

New York's famous landmarks — Times Square, Madison Avenue, Central Park and finally, the imposing facade of the Metropolitan Museum bedecked with enormous banners.

We started our tour in the new Michael Rockefeller Wing, built to house a magnificent collection of traditional Melanesian art forms, many collected by the late Michael Rockefeller Jr during his last fatal journey to the Asmat. With the Fifth Avenue skyline silhouetted through the gallery's huge rear glass wall, the aesthetic effect created by the objects in this vast architectural setting is highly dramatic.

Leaving Melanesia behind, we walked on to view other artistic creations from civilisations unfamiliar to Larry — tribal Africa, Ancient Egypt and the Americas, Classical Greece and Rome and displays of European art from the early Renaissance to the shimmering and colorful image of the impressionists and post-impressionists. Although too many images in one encounter can overwhelm the senses, I hoped that Larry would leave the Metropolitan feeling that artistically he was connected to an elaborate and enduring tradition of human creativity.

We were up early on our first morning in Bridgewater because

**Next page, top** *Painting by Grade 2 schoolgirl, Lynne Stevens inspired by contemporary PNG art on display at Bridgewater.* **bottom** *Painting by Grade 4 pupil, Andrea Estes, similarly inspired.*

the Art and Anthropology faculty were bringing their morning classes to the gallery and Larry and I were asked to speak informally about the PNG art on display. As well as meeting these students, Larry attended a Life Drawing class and participated in working with a professional model. This was a new experience for Larry

who, welcomed and encouraged by the students, worked alongside them with easy rapport. With obvious interest, they asked many questions about his life in PNG and, naturally, everyone also wanted to know Larry's reactions to being in the USA. Trying to sum up such enormous contrasts, I heard him say several times: "Oh, it is so different here, I feel I am dreaming."

The highpoint of the day came that evening with the official opening of the exhibition. This included a reception and my introductory slide lecture, which provided a context for the art on display. I pointed out that many people consider art a universal language which automatically stimulates an aesthetic response in its viewers. However, the contemporary art of PNG is not just 'art for art's sake', but reflects the problems, conflicting values and aspirations of a new nation undergoing rapid social change.

Larry Santana, like other new artists in PNG, is a social critic; his intricate symbolic images reflect pride in the fundamental value of traditional village life and express pain at the confusion and contention of culture clash.

For example, Immiwang, Bird of Warning — one of Larry's exhibition drawings — illustrates a legend from his mother's people that symbolizes the dependence of humans upon creatures of the natural world. When interpreted in a contemporary context, however, Immiwang also warns of the need to protect the natural environment from the threats of invasive destruction.

Larry's 1988 self-portrait, Struggle and Pain at the Six-Mile Dump, selected for the cover of the Bridgewater Exhibition Catalogue, expresses the pain and suffering of being unemployed in the city with a young family to support. Although this image is personal, the predicaments of hunger, dislocation and social alienation which it depicts affect many others in Port Moresby and throughout the world. Larry Santana's art therefore addresses us all.

# compensation

# CEREMONY

Story and photographs by Nancy Cohen

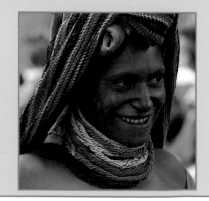

M y visit to Papua New Guinea became one of my life's most exciting experiences when I was invited, along with two travelling companions, to attend a compensation ceremony near Mendi, in the Highlands. The young man who invited us worked at our gatehouse and knew we were searching for adventure.

We asked what a compensation ceremony was. He explained that one of his clan had been killed in a car accident. Formerly this could have provoked war, causing loss of life and possibly lasting for a long time. In recent times, however, economic compensation has come to prevail. The clan suffering the loss of a member is compensated by the clan of the offending party. The compensation takes the form of money, pigs, birds, cuscus — just about anything considered currency.

This explanation did not prepare me for the enormous treat in store for us. We boarded a truck for a long, bumpy trip and by the time we reached the ceremony, there were several thousand people massing. As the only outsiders, the temptation to wander freely among these colorful people was too much to resist.

Surrounding an area about as large as a sports arena, people sat or stood in groups. In the centre a small gathering of what seemed to be organ-

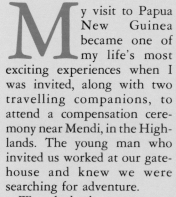

isers or leaders were apparently discussing the events which were about to take place. Women were adorned in their finest beads, often matching their clothing. Children were carried on shoulders. Amid welcoming smiles, I found I was as interesting to the local people as they were to me.

A large group of men caught my attention. They wore great headdresses of beads and feathers and were carrying spears and axes. Their nearly naked, muscular bodies were well-oiled, and their faces were painted in bright colors I've come to associate with PNG.

Loud chanting began among a large group of the clan which was bearing the compensation, or paying. Several people carried large boards covered with rows of paper money made into colorful signs. Others were gathered around someone who was shouting. A row of pigs' quarters neatly laid out on the ground in front of him was part of the compensation.

Near the chanting group I saw a group of men who formed a procession — six men across and eleven rows long — and danced around in a circle. Children watched them, fascinated by their colorful elders. When the procession stopped, the leader delivered instructions.

Friendly faces became serious and a large procession began to form from all the groups preparing for the

*Facing page* Both sides come armed but the mood is friendly, albeit a little apprehensive as shown by the woman at **bottom left**. **This page** Compensation ceremonies call for traditional dress but non-traditional paper money **(left)** is acceptable.

ceremony. Men carried pigs' quarters on their shoulders; others carried money signs above their head. In front of the procession was the flag of PNG, followed by poles to which a cuscus and an eagle had been tied. A man walked behind a cassowary bird.

The chanting became louder as the procession grew. Excitement was mounting. The compensation recipients were all seated in the centre of the circle of marching warriors. As the parade of fierce compensation payers circled around and around, they chanted, raised weapons, and displayed their wealth for all to see.

After speeches were delivered, compensation approved and received, the excitement wound down. We were on our way back to Mt Hagen, having experienced a fascinating part of PNG's ancient culture which is adapting to the face of new ways such as the use of money for compensation.

Air Niugini operates regular services to Mendi from Port Moresby.

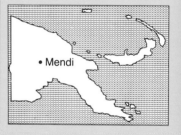

• Mendi

**Top** *National flag flying over proceedings is another modern touch but traditional sides of pig* **(bottom right)** *remain the basis of compensation.*

# Dream Fishing

Story and photographs
by Dean Butler

When a sport-fisherman day-dreams about faraway, exotic locations and untapped, unspoilt sportfish, the list of areas is fairly short and getting shorter.

Sportfishermen are a strange lot who will travel the world in pursuit of a particular species. They will spend thousands of dollars to catch a fish bigger than anyone else. Talk to serious travel-orientated sportfishermen and they will all tell you that the areas they go to fish are usually the most beautiful and untouched places left on earth.

**Left** *Barracuda with the lure it found irresistible.*

31

**Below left** *A 320kg black marlin clears the water.* **below, right** *Spanish mackerel ready for the landing net.* **facing page, from left** *Chris O'Keefe and trevally; Rod Harrison and 25kg barramundi; apprentice Kulu River guide and clients.*

Sportfishermen practise catch and release, that is to say they are quite happy to return all fish to the water, unharmed. This means that the sportfish are a reusable resource. Such fishing has a low impact on the culture and the people of any given area and, properly managed, has no harmful effect on the environment. It does, however, create local employment opportunities.

What has PNG to offer the sportfishing world? Being a very young country geologically, it has many major river systems pouring millions of litres of fresh water into the ocean every day. The waters surrounding most of PNG are also some of the deepest in the world and are favored with rich ocean currents that carry an enormous amount of oceanic life.

There is a very important link between the freshwater flow of rivers and the blue water that surrounds them. The basic food chain needed for any aquatic life to survive starts in the estuary. This is the nursery, where mangroves play a very important role in supporting many of the tiny creatures that the smaller estuary fish live on. These small fish become a major food source for larger fish and in turn attract the larger predators that are of most interest to the sportfisherman. This food chain ends up way out at sea, where great gamefish such as marlin and tuna can be found. All these factors make PNG a prime location for pristine sportfishing.

Nearly all of the major fish species found in the South Pacific are found in PNG. Two of the most powerful river-dwelling fish can be found nowhere else. They are the PNG black bass and the spot tail bass.

The barramundi, which is widely distributed around the 'top end' of Australia, is found in most of the Papuan Rivers running south into the Gulf of Papua. One of the best, and the only one reasonably accessible to people travelling to PNG, is the Bensbach River. It is a big, fish-rich water course, meandering through lowland forest and lush waving grassland, finding its slow way to the sea near the Irian Jaya border.

Less than 100km inland from the river mouth is the Bensbach Wildlife Lodge. Its deceptively simple design harmonising perfectly with its surroundings, it offers a well-equipped, comfortable base from which anglers can enjoy world-class fishing for lagoon barramundi.

The other land-based fishing lodge in PNG is the Kulu River bass fishing lodge located in West New Britain and run by Sportfishing Adventures. It is where sportfishermen can be guided in the pursuit of the native PNG black bass and spot tail bass.

The bass is the classic ambush feeder, hiding behind logs or anything that deflects current and waiting for small fish, or any other creature to come past. They come out of cover at lightning speed, turn on the chosen prey and on the way back to the cover strike the fish or lure with such force that they can quite often break the 18kg line that is needed to catch them in a straight pull.

This is the challenge for the angler. There is not a trick in the book that bass will not use to escape.

Black bass are found in the brackish tidal sections of the lower end of the rivers down to

the mouth. The spot tail is found in the faster, upper reaches and both fish have the strength to give any angler a hard time.

The Kulu River camp has proved to be quite successful and should produce stunning sport-fishing for years to come. Other fish species encountered there include mangrove jack, giant trevally, queenfish and finger-mark bream. Outside the river mouth, clients fish for spanish mackerel, trevally, barracuda and many other species that put a bend in a fishing rod.

As good as the fishery is on the Kulu, sportfishermen are always looking for something better.

Sportfishing Adventures, with the support of Air Niugini, put together an exploratory trip that took them down the remote south coast of New Britain. From the research they did and after many hours poring over maps, they believe that this area has the potential to be one of the greatest sportfishing destinations.

It would appear from what they have learned, there will be plenty of opportunities for anglers to pursue gamefish such as blue and black marlin, sailfish, wahoo, various tuna species, and numerous reef dwelling fish such as spanish mackerel, coral trout and giant trevally. Add to it the fact that there are hundreds of unfished rivers and creeks which should be loaded with the black and spot tail bass, all in an unspoilt environment. It makes for the sort of fishing of which dreams are made.

# TIDIKAWA
## REVISITED

**Story and photographs
by David Eastburn**

In the late 1960s a film was made about the Biami people who live near Nomad River in the Western Province. It was named 'Tidikawa', in honor of one of the main characters, a young spirit medium who conducted seances to contact ancestor spirits.

The Biami are forest dwellers whose territory occupies part of the Great Papuan Plateau. The film recorded their traditional lifestyle, which at the time was little influenced by Western society or the industrialised world. In the late 1960s the Biami, who were the dominant group in the region, still greatly resented the imposition of Australian administration laws on their lives. Many government laws were totally opposite to traditional Biami values, which created tension and the potential for conflict.

While making the film, the crew came to know the people of Obeimi village quite well and over the years often thought of them. They wondered what various individuals might be doing and how the lifestyle of the Biami people might have changed. From these idle thoughts grew the idea of a second film to show the changes which have occurred in the past 20 years.

**Right** *Biami initiates in traditional stripes of yellow ochre and wearing bark wigs.* **inset** *Missionary Tom Hoey greets one of his flock at market.*

After years of planning, Susan Cornwell, who had assisted with the making of the original 'Tidikawa' film and who was now a film director, returned to the land of the Biami to convert a dream into reality.

During the long flight from Port Moresby, she tried to imagine what she would find. Susan had contacted Tom and Salome Hoey, missionaries who had established a mission station at Mougulu in Biami territory in the early 1970s. Nothing could have prepared her for what she was about to experience.

Finally, below, in the heart of Biami territory was Mougulu. This hydro-powered settlement consists of mission buildings, a school, a church community centre, a hospital, a sports field, a trade store, dairy sheds and a sawmill clustered around the airstrip.

A welcoming committee, complete with a sign in colored chalk, gathered around the aircraft. Susan was overwhelmed. She had expected to have to search for the people from Obeimi, not to have them waiting to welcome her.

Following a welcome by Tom Hoey and a short discussion, Susan was reintroduced to Tidikawa. Although 20 years older and dressed in a pair of shorts and a t-shirt, he had changed very little. Others pushed forward to be reintroduced. The people from Obeimi had been told by the Hoeys that Susan was returning to make another film and they eagerly awaited her arrival.

The new film was given the working title of 'Tidikawa Revisited'. Susan was the director, as well as an actress. Cameraman Steve Mason had worked on many films including 'Mad Max' and 'Gorillas in the Mist'. Soundman Ian

**Top** Susan shows villager photograph of himself taken 20 years ago. **bottom** Susan's welcoming committee of Biami people.

*Top* Mougulu's sole land transport vehicle. **centre** Soundman Ian Sherrey and cameraman Steve Mason during a break in filming. **bottom** Tom Hoey talking to Mougulu villagers.

Sherrey had recently worked on a film called 'Passage out of Paradise', about a race between small sailing canoes from Bali, in Indonesia, to Melville Island in Northern Australia.

The main characters in 'Tidikawa Revisited' quickly emerged. They were Tidikawa; Haiefi, who had been Tidikawa's seance assistant in the first film; and Tom and Salome Hoey, who had brought Christianity and many other changes to the lives of the Biami.

Tidikawa has resisted many of the changes brought by the mission. He still contacts the ancestor spirits and follows many traditional Biami beliefs. Haiefi has become a Christian and is an active member of the mission community.

Susan brought with her a large collection of photographs taken during the making of the first film. These created great interest — the people living around Mougulu never tired of looking at them. Visitors from surrounding areas also often arrived to view these images from the past. More exciting than the photographs were videos of the original Tidikawa film and other footage taken at the same time. Video evenings at the community centre were extremely popular.

As the film progressed, the changes which had taken place in Biami society over the past 20 years became obvious. Biami longhouses are still built on ridges with commanding views over the surrounding countryside, but they no longer serve as fortresses. Gone are the loopholes, slotted at intervals along the walls, which enabled the inhabitants to fire arrows at the enemy. The fighting platforms at the rear of the houses are now recreational meeting places. The paths are no longer booby-trapped with needle-sharp skewers to puncture the feet of would-be attackers. Today, some Biamis, especially Christians, live in individual family houses.

Biami dead are no longer placed on platforms next to the longhouses. This custom was forbidden as a health hazard by the Australian administration. Burial was very difficult for the Biami to accept, as they believed that the ground was inhabited by evil spirits.

**Top** *Salome Hoey talking with Obeimi villagers.* **centre** *Biami mother and daughter at initiation ceremony.* **bottom** *Biami warriors were always well armed and prepared to defend themselves.*

Today, coconut trees are sometimes planted near graves, although tradition prevented the Biami from growing coconuts in the past. They believed that the earth would turn upside down if coconut trees were planted by Biami people.

Songs sung in the longhouses today may be traditional ballads, 'spirit singing', or Christian hymns which have been translated into Biami language. 'Amazing Grace' is a favorite. Traditional initiation ceremonies are still carried out, but today 'initiation' for young people includes going to school.

Probably the most significant change in Biami society has been in the area of communication. People can now travel freely and without fear. Aircraft regularly visit Mougulu. Radios bring the rest of PNG to the Biami. Young Biami people can communicate with people in other parts of the country and overseas. A computer has recently been installed at Mougulu to assist with the recording of the Bible in the Biami language. Peace, Christianity and a cash economy have all brought great changes to Biami society.

The Biami have adopted some Western ideas and products and dropped some traditional customs, but remain proud of their culture. The new film has now been edited and includes segments from the original 'Tidikawa' combined with footage about the Biami people today. The new film has been named 'Tidikawa — At The Edge Of Heaven'. This raises the possibility of a third film — perhaps 'Tidikawa 2010', being produced to record the changes in the lives of the Biami people over the next 20 years.

Story and Photographs by Liz Thompson

# BUSH

# JEWELLERY

Jan Barter has lived in Papua New Guinea almost 20 years, spending much of that time on the Sepik River, running the Melanesian Explorer and the newer boat, the Melanesian Discoverer. Her incredible jewellery collection bears witness, not only to her appreciation and knowledge of local craft and customs but also to newer, more sophisticated jewellery production aided by modern technology.

Walking through Tambanum village, surrounded by children, she wears three pieces which represent three, quite different types of contemporarily produced jewellery. On her finger is an old PNG penny, moulded onto a band and worn as a ring. It was made by Kara Jewellers in Port Moresby. Around her neck is a dog tooth necklace made in Soi village on the Karawari River and around her upper arm is a delicately carved boar's tusk made by Jeff Liverseidge. He is a local resident who lives near Ambunti on the Sepik River and produces much of his jewellery using an assortment of fine dentist's drills.

Traditional local jewellery is still produced but more store beads and synthetic materials are being incorporated into the designs. Rather than simply being made for the purpose of self adornment, jewellery is frequently made for sale. It has become a source of income for many villagers.

The Kina shell, or gold lipped pearl shell, is one of the most significant adornments. Usually hung from bush rope made of rolled aerial roots of the pandanus palm, the Sepiks wear it dished up, so that the natural curve moves away from the body. Highlanders wear it turned inwards. Small cowries are sometimes sewn to the rope and the shell often displays a wonderful patina from repeated wear, either rubbed a shiny, rich, golden yellow or a deep red as it swings against skin smeared with oil and clays.

Sepik mourning necklaces are still made and sold commercially. Traditionally put on the body of the dead, removed and given to the next of kin they also serve as part of the currency system, representing the toea, PNG's smallest monetary denomination. Small round kina shells represent Kina, the basic unit of PNG currency. Threaded onto bark they are usually worn as belts or bracelets. Often made in Palambei on the Sepik, they are becoming increasingly rare and many have been sold off since coinage replaced shell money.

**Title page** *Goroka woman with decoration.* **below** *Gold lip kina shell necklace.*

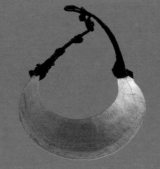

As well as shells, parts of animal are often used for decoration. Thin black quills of the cassowary spine, like licorice, are wound around the neck. Swordfish spine is cut up and threaded onto string. One of Jan's most interesting pieces is made from a snake vertebra. Kept whole it has been smoothed and threaded onto a choker. Boar and pig tusks are often used traditionally but usually as nose pieces, not something that would appeal to many from a western culture.

Dog teeth, flying fox teeth and pig teeth are threaded to make necklaces and bracelets. Sometimes pieces of bone or teeth are separated by wild seed — the small, shiny black seed of the wild banana palm or the round, yellow lattice etched seed of the sago palm. Small grey seeds, known locally as Job's tears are used in the Highlands as a sign of mourning. On the Sepik they have a purely decorative purpose, threaded with cowrie shells and sago seeds to make huge three or four-inch deep chokers.

Quite different but using almost exactly the same 'bush materials' is the work produced by jewellery maker, Jeff Liverseidge. Having been settled in PNG for many years he lives in the bush on the banks of the Sepik. He makes many unique pieces which are becoming increasingly popular despite his obvious lack of interest in advertising. Many of the most beautiful pieces in Jan's collection have been made by Jeff. One of the finest is a cameo, carved from shell and surrounded by tiny green feathers and cowries.

Perhaps the river's most common bird is the beautiful white egret that flies unexpectedly from the surrounding grasslands. Jeff's trademark is the egret he delicately carves from crocodile teeth, mounting them in silver or gold, sometimes using tortoiseshell caps to make earrings or necklaces.

Examples of his work are numerous. Bright, emerald green snail shells from Manus make wonderful earrings. The foot, or operculum (door) of the turban shell is worked onto tortoiseshell tear drops and hang from a necklace. A present Jan received was a piece Jeff called 'A Memory of Sepik and Ramu Art'. A choker made of local bark and covered with tiny cowries, it holds five charms. On the left and right are Sepik hooks or 'wanleg' made of boar's tusk. In between there are three wooden masks; on the far right

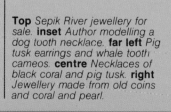

*Top* Sepik River jewellery for sale. **inset** *Author modelling a dog tooth necklace.* **far left** *Pig tusk earrings and whale tooth cameos.* **centre** *Necklaces of black coral and pig tusk.* **right** *Jewellery made from old coins and coral and pearl.*

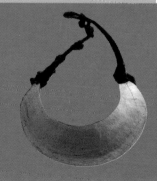

one from Swagup, the Upper Sepik, the two others from the Ramu River.

All made from local materials, the choker celebrates local art while being different from anything that was produced by the villagers. He has carved also a figure from one piece of black coral with tiny earrings and a necklace that actually turn. Another was cut from ebony wood, both represent female Sepik spirits from Mindimbit village.

One step further removed and quite different again is the jewellery made by Kara Jewellers in Moresby. Using many local materials, their work is influenced in its design by local product but follows a more western tradition. Necklaces of red and black coral, and tiny pearls line their display cases and sell in many of the country's major hotels. Pig tusk is cut and mounted with silver caps and linked to form bracelets. Jan has commissioned a lot of her jewellery through Kara, including a beautiful cameo, made from whale's tooth, hanging from a thin gold chain. Another commission was a choker which holds a golden bird of paradise, one of PNG's most famous birds, here laced with precious stones. Kara Jewellery, although far away from village decoration and bush materials, incorporates local materials such as corals, pearls, pig tusks and occasionally, as in the case of the bird of paradise, local symbols.

These are not the only kinds of jewellery in PNG, but between them they provide an interesting cross section. Traditional body adornment made

in the villages, some for purely decorative purposes, some for ceremonial purposes, is still produced though more frequently using elements of synthetic materials now available in the stores.

Jeff's work is beautifully intricate and while using predominantly bush materials, the use of fine drills allows him to describe very fine detail. Kara Jewellers display a very much more refined product using elements of local material in conjunction with imported products and occasionally using local imagery as an influence in their designs. Together they illustrate the traditional methods of body adornment and local craft and the changes taking place through the advent of technology of which Jeff's pieces are a stunning example.

**Top** *Tourists shopping for Sepik River jewellery.* **left** *Headband and traditional belt of cowries.* **bottom** *Sea shell belt and bracelet.*

# Return of the Golden
# COWRIE

Story and photographs by Peter Stone

It was Skeeter who found the first one. He wasn't exactly jumping up and down with joy about it and seemed quite reluctant at first to show it to anyone. But his pride eventually overcame his shyness and with a beaming smile he produced the ultimate find of the shell collector — a golden cowrie.

Skeeter had gone off on his own for a dive while we were anchored off Eagle Ray Pass, marked on the charts as Planet Channel between Enang Island and Nuselawa Island on the south-east corner of the New Hanover, Papua New Guinea. We had several dives in this spot, reputed for its excellent pelagic marine life and of course eagle rays. But we saw none during the half-dozen dives we did in the region. Even so, the diving was superb with gorgonia and sea whips covering the sloping walls of the pass entrance.

Skeeter's golden cowrie was found on the sandy bottom of the channel in 30 metres of water. Skeeter had moved off from the wall and by chance had swum over the shell lying fully exposed on the sand. He

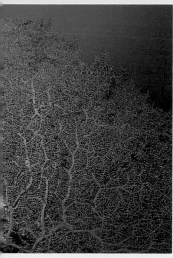

recognised it immediately.

We were diving from Bob and Dinah Halstead's magnificent 20-metre dive cruiser, Telita. Skeeter is one of Bob's deckhands, a delightful 21-year-old from Logia near Samurai in Milne Bay province whom Bob taught to dive when he joined the Telita in Madang in 1986.

"That's typical!" Bob said in his usual humorous way. "You teach the guy to dive and look what he finds." In 20 years of diving in PNG Bob has yet to find a golden cowrie.

Needless to say everyone on board was delighted with Skeeter's good fortune — and somewhat envious I should add.

Most of the divers on board were from Port Moresby and between them had an excellent knowledge of shells. Trish Quayle, a physiology lecturer at the College of Applied Health and Sciences in Port Moresby, was our resident expert and over the 10 days that we were on board the Telita I learnt more about shells than in the past 10 years looking through books.

The golden cowrie is mag-

**Above** *Golden cowries.* **top right** *New Hanover sunset.* **bottom right** *Clown fish and anemone on the wreck of the Taisyo Maru.*

nificent. Although not the rarest of the cowries, nor the most valuable, Cypraea aurantium is arguably the most beautiful. It has indeed a golden lustre to it, deepening in color from the lip to dorsum or upper region. They are usually found in caves and underhangs in about five to 20 metres. Skeeter's find on the open seabed was all the more unusual as they are rarely found exposed. The point that must be emphasised is that Skeeter's golden cowrie did not have a live animal inside. How long the dead shell lay on the seabed is anyone's guess but the excellent condition of the shell suggests that it had not been long rolling around on the sand otherwise it would have been badly scarred and encrusted.

According to an authority on the subject, C. M. Burgess, in his magnificent 'Cowries of the World', Cypraea aurantium are found throughout the central Pacific, with Fiji apparently being the centre of population. They are known to have been found in the Solomons but not so many have been recorded in PNG.

Yet the going price of a good golden cowrie appears to be incongruous with its rarity, according to Burgess. "Cypraea aurantium is priced out of all proportion to its rarity simply because of the tremendous popular demand. It is a mystery to me why the price of the cowrie should remain so high when possibly 2,000 have been collected. I guess they are simply so large and beautiful that everyone has to have one."

Indeed we do. The going price for a fine specimen is from K250 to K400.

After Skeeter's prize find there seemed to be an even greater keenness to be kitted up and down under at every opportunity. Of course no one expected any more of these jewels of the sea to be found, particularly as Bob was still shaking his head in bewilderment. So imagine the reaction three days later when another beautiful specimen was found.

Peer Kirkemo could not believe his luck. We were diving in a site called Peter's Patch, one of the nicest reefs in the southern channel between New Hanover and New Ireland. Visibility was the

usual 30 metres; the reef extends from about six metres down a sloping edge to about 30 metres. Peer found his golden cowrie within 20 metres of the anchor, under a plate coral. It was another dead shell with no animal inside.

Gold fever seemed to spread throughout the boat when Peer emerged with his find. Virtually everyone on board was a photographer but on the next dive only a few divers took their cameras down. The hunt was on. Bob was one of the first in the water. I still took my Nikonos down but I must admit that I spent most of my time up-ended under plate corals and grovelling in holes.

One of the most experienced divers on board was Australian Rick Warnett, another knowledgeable shell collector and keen photographer who was having his second trip on the Telita. A computer technician living in Port Moresby since 1975, Rick has been diving for more than 17 years.

Having a logical and technical mind, Rick knew he had little hope of finding a golden cowrie of his own but he was determined to at least try. No one was more surprised than he when he found the third golden cowrie of the trip on a ledge under a large coral outcrop. With some bewilderment at his incredible luck, Rick took the shell over to Trish who was diving nearby. His joy turned to frustration when Trish pointed out that the shell was alive. The mantle was well withdrawn inside the shell but there was no doubt about it; Rick had found a live Cypraea aurantium.

We were astounded at the incredible luck of having found three golden cowries all within three days, and the last two within a matter of hours and on the same reef. But to some, life itself has a far greater value than the materialistic reward of an inanimate object. As much as Rick wanted to add a golden cowrie to his shell collection, his affinity with marine life and his integrity in keeping within his moral values led him to an important decision. He would put the live shell back in exactly the place where he found it.

The shell was placed in a bucket of seawater while we had lunch, to allow it sufficient surface interval so it could be returned safely to the site. A dark towel was placed over the bucket in the hope that the shell would extend its mantle.

According to Burgess: "the animal is brilliant dark-to-orange brown, mottled throughout and intensified on all sides toward the mantle edge. The mantle is thick, covered with hundreds of white, round tuberclelike papillae. The siphon bears a short scalloped fringe. The tentacles are light brown-orange, two centimetres in length, and taper to a fine blue point which is almost black. The foot is orange-yellow, the edge almost white, smooth, with no spotting."

We had to accept Burgess' description as our specimen would not be fooled into thinking it was night.

Two hours later, Rick's golden cowrie was back where it came from.

Postscript: Four weeks after the Telita trip I had the good fortune to find my own golden cowrie, on a wreck in the Solomon Islands. There was no live animal inside.

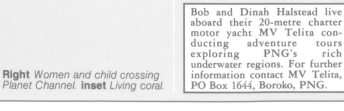

**Right** Women and child crossing Planet Channel. **inset** Living coral.

Bob and Dinah Halstead live aboard their 20-metre charter motor yacht MV Telita conducting adventure tours exploring PNG's rich underwater regions. For further information contact MV Telita, PO Box 1644, Boroko, PNG.

ory by Rani Hesketh. Photographs by Greg Bluett

**Top** *Dawn in Rabaul as the sun rises behind Matupit, the 'mother' volcano.* **bottom** *In full daylight cloud gathers at Matupit summit.*

# R·A·B·A·U·L

Nestled on Simpson Harbor, Rabaul has withstood two World Wars and numerous volcanic holocausts, yet retains a mystical beauty that takes one's breath away.

Dawn over Simpson Harbor was a spiritual experience for us on our first morning in Rabaul. The sun appeared to grow out of the 'mother' volcano which although dormant is impressive for its sheer size. As the sun began to glow and paint the sky pink and blue, the many birds awoke and chattered.

After breakfast we drove to the hot springs at the base of the 'mother' and 'daughter' volcanoes. Here the ocean is boiling and the steam billows eerily across orange rocks, iron oxidised by the heat. Great colors for photography but havoc on lenses and cameras. Greg

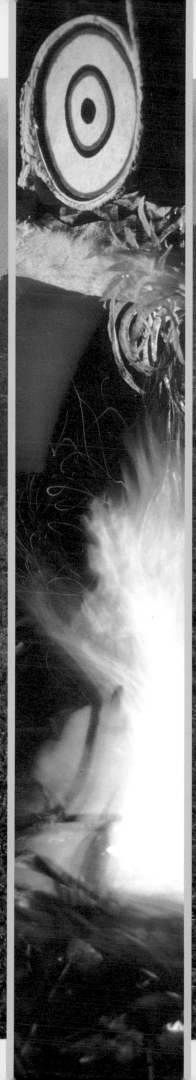

slipped on a rock and could have seriously scalded his foot if he had not worn good thick sneakers. Blocks of concrete are the only evidence of baths built here by the Japanese during World War II. We learned from our guide, Boas, that the villagers here collect wild fowl eggs at the base of Matupit volcano and cook them in the hot, salty water. It sounded delicious.

We dashed back to the airport to rendezvous with our helicopter which took us on a journey to a live volcano. We deposited Greg on the edge of the crater to photograph us as we flew right into the yellow steam issuing from vents to the centre of the earth.

This was my first time in a helicopter and the sensation was stunning. I felt perfectly safe even though the doors had been taken off.

Skimming the abundant palm trees

we headed out over the harbor to the 'beehives', two huge columns of rock thrusting out of the water. The 'beehives' are all that remain of a solid rock core of an ancient and gigantic volcanic crater that is in fact Simpson Harbor. The 'hives' are ringed by superb layered reefs.

We flew out of the harbor and over a World War II Japanese submarine base. Here the coral face drops steeply to the edge of the continental shelf and at low tide several large tunnels are revealed. During the war, Japanese submarines berthed here for supplies as the cove was well hidden and protected by several gun emplacements. The clarity and color of the water was almost surreal and I was tempted to dive from the helicopter and let the cool waters engulf me.

Later that day we explored and photographed more Japanese tunnels. In one, my imagination turned some bleached coral into human bones and we heard murmuring voices which to my relief turned out to be fellow explorers.

Over the course of the next few days we photographed dolphins chasing our boat, a symphony of synchronised swimming. We struggled out of bed to witness one amazing

dawn after the other, had our first scuba dive with the patient Frank Butler as instructor, walked barefoot on brilliant white sandy beaches, explored seemingly endless caves and tunnels, and experienced the evidence of history. Yet try as we might we just could not seem to take it all in. There is just so much to see and do in Rabaul.

The Bainings fire dancers were the

highlight of our week. After a steep night drive we arrived at a small village where fire flies blinked in the trees. Distant lightning and a full moon heralded a mystical night.

When the drummers began, from the dark emerged a lone dancer, later joined by seven more. As the fire built up, one by one the dancers leaped into it and were shrouded by flames. As they emerged the grass fronds around their ankles were still burning and they stamped furiously in the damp grass. I was mesmerised and when the time came to leave I wanted only to stay and the dance to continue.

At the end of one week we had to leave this beautiful and peaceful town. After seeing the results of our visit on film, we were determined to return.

**Top left** *In spite of appearances Matupit is dormant.* **bottom left** *Rabaul nestles on Simpson Harbor, itself a caldera.* **right** *Bainings fire dancer.*

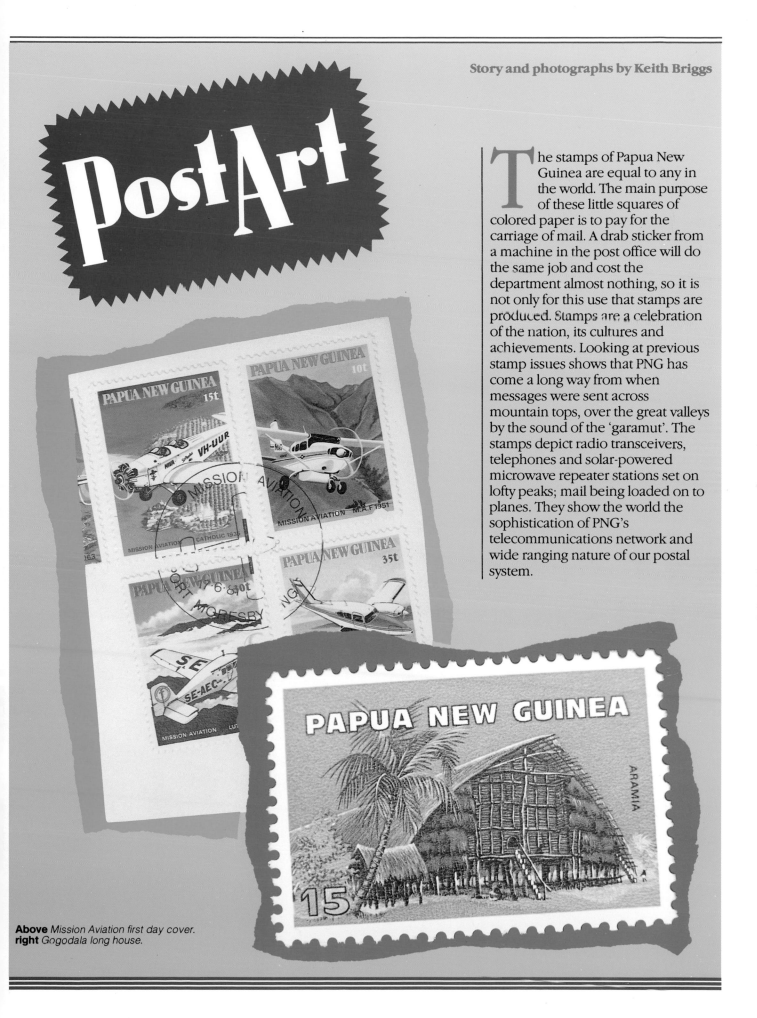

# PostArt

**Story and photographs by Keith Briggs**

The stamps of Papua New Guinea are equal to any in the world. The main purpose of these little squares of colored paper is to pay for the carriage of mail. A drab sticker from a machine in the post office will do the same job and cost the department almost nothing, so it is not only for this use that stamps are produced. Stamps are a celebration of the nation, its cultures and achievements. Looking at previous stamp issues shows that PNG has come a long way from when messages were sent across mountain tops, over the great valleys by the sound of the 'garamut'. The stamps depict radio transceivers, telephones and solar-powered microwave repeater stations set on lofty peaks; mail being loaded on to planes. They show the world the sophistication of PNG's telecommunications network and wide ranging nature of our postal system.

**Above** *Mission Aviation first day cover.*
**right** *Gogodala long house.*

Momentous events like self government, Independence or the opening of the new Parliament House were shared with many nations via our stamps. The nutrition stamp issue had a valuable purpose in educating people of the need for a balanced diet. A centenary celebration, recognition of the police force, the army and the scouting movement have each been depicted. An issue honoring early missionaries reminded modern citizens that these people ventured into isolated areas, to settle, learn local languages and open schools and medical services, while spreading the Gospel, the only message able to unite people of more than 700 languages and cultures. They built airstrips in difficult places and even today the only contact for hundreds of small groups is by Mission Aviation.

Some countries produce stamps depicting things outside their own land and have resorted to many

**Left** *Artist Graham Wade at work.*
**above** *First day cover celebrating traditional buildings.*

approaches to sell stamps. PNG has resisted this gimmick and has maintained a policy of producing serious stamps relevant to the country. They retain a photographic quality and accuracy rather than using cartoon figures, line drawings or abstract subjects. Because of this, our stamps are highly regarded and eagerly sought by collectors around the world.

Most of us buy our sheets of stamps without thinking about how they were produced. Information printed in the sheet margins gives some clues.

One name that often appears is G. Wade. Graham is a commercial designer and has directed films and videos for the Philatelic Bureau, Standards Australia, Jones Lang Wootton, APCM, African Enterprise and the Bible Society, through his firm Pilgrim International. He lives with his family in a quiet bushland setting in a northern suburb of Sydney.

Graham is one of several artists who play a large part in the production of PNG stamps. A request from the Philatelic Bureau sets him researching picture books to get inspiration and accuracy for the proposed theme. Sometimes he will work out a series on his own, producing rough sketches about twice the size of the finished article. If the concept is approved by the bureau, it is sent to the Stamp Advisory Board who approve and return it. Working initially with the artist, the Bureau then has the job of producing and distributing millions of stamps.

Up to two years is needed from the initial sketch to the First Day when the public sees the new issue. A tremendous amount of organisation goes into getting an issue out to coincide with coming events, such as the opening of Parliament House or the Queen's visit.

If approval is given on submitted sketches, Graham produces a painting about five times the size the stamp will be, in the correct proportions. A clear sheet of film is

**Top** *Artist Graham Wade.*
**bottom** *A typical Wade design.*

laid over the finished painting and the wording, denomination and artwork such as the Scout badge, are reproduced in black rather than on the painting's surface. Graham regularly checks the picture through reducing glasses to see it in the exact size it will be printed. Visual gaps must be left so they can join in pleasing proportion in the final reduced product. Four designs are usually submitted but perhaps only two will be chosen.

The Swiss firm of Courvoisier prints a large percentage of the PNG stamps. The two favored printing processes used are gravure and litho. Printing by the best firms is expensive but it pays off in high quality stamps with the vibrant colors we all know.

Because they are literally printing money, the printers have to observe tight security. All stamp sheets are carefully checked and the presses are sealed overnight to prevent some enterprising employee running off a few after hours! The printing plates are sealed and carefully guarded; they are

**Top** *Marking 75 years of Scouts in PNG.* **above and right** *Initial rough sketches for submission to Philatelic Bureau.*

58

destroyed once the issue is completed. The delivery of stamps from the printers must be by security consignment. As release dates have been publicised, all post offices must have supplies by that date. The logistics of distribution alone are quite a feat. With the stamps are First Day covers, pre-stamped envelopes, presentation stamp packs and stamp folders. Graham has several of these as well as aerograms to his credit, and he has produced Christmas cards for the Post and Telecommunication Corporation.

PNG's world class stamps truly are model ambassadors. They are attractive, do their job well, are highly respected and admired wherever they travel and are eagerly welcomed into the homes of those who meet them. To overseas friends who know PNG, they surely must bring back the scent of frangipani, the song of the birds and the never-to-be-forgotten voices of children singing: "Jungles and rivers, white coral sands, this is my country, this is my land".

**Top** First day cover for Self Government in 1973. **above** Annual stamp pack cover shows Port Moresby (top) and Rabaul. **left** Douglas and Campbell Briggs, at school in Queensland, receive mail from home in PNG.

# silvertip SHARKS

Story and photographs by Bob Halstead

From June to November the south-east trade winds bring clear skies and calm weather to the waters of New Hanover and northern New Ireland. These fair conditions and the excellent diving that we have experienced in previous visits, tempt us each year to cruise north from our home base at Alotau in Milne Bay in our 20-metre dive charter vessel MV Telita.

We are lucky to have been the first divers to systematically explore underwater the exquisite virgin reefs of this idyllic part of Papua New Guinea. It was on one of these untouched reefs that we discovered one of the most exciting dives in all of my 17 years of diving in PNG.

As we prepared to explore the reef, probably to be the first humans to see its secrets, I looked around at my fellow divers and sensed the joy of adventure that we were sharing.

The water was very clear and it was easy to see the sandy slope from the top of the coral reef. Myriads of exotic tropical fishes were flashing a kaleidoscope of rainbow colors. But no grey reef sharks. This was strange.

**Left** *Shark expert Valerie Taylor hand feeding a silvertip shark, an activity not recommended by the author.* **inset** *Master of the deep, a silvertip with distinctively colored dorsal fin.*

Soon however some sharks did appear but instead of the ubiquitous grey reef they were the magnificent silvertip shark, *Carcharhinus albimarginatus*. This shark is often seen in PNG, particularly on the outer reef walls near very deep water. It is a large shark growing to three metres, and has a big girth. It has a light bronze color and is distinguished by brilliant silver edges to its fins.

**Left** *A silvertip making a close pass by Dinah Halstead.* **below** *A silvertip moving in for a closer look at Valerie Taylor.*

When you see a silvertip you know you are seeing a real shark! One of diving's greatest moments is to be looking out into the blue water on an outer reef and notice silver lights weaving their way up from the deep. As the shark nears, the rest of its shape becomes apparent. It prefers a direct approach and will move straight towards you veering off only at the last moment, a little unnerving for the uninitiated. Those in the know stay still and hold their breath. Then the shark will come within touching distance before turning and swimming away.

Several silvertip sharks swam around the reef, but there was not a sign of any grey reef sharks. After the dive, Dinah and I started thinking of the possibilities. We had never been in a situation where we were able to feed the silvertip shark without grey reefs coming in and making the feed chaotic. When the silvertips were involved, the grey reefs seemed to agitate them. The grey reefs, although smaller, always managed to get the baits before the silvertips. Here we had a very unusual situation where we had silvertips without any grey reefs; what would happen if we started to feed them? Returning to New Ireland for our next charter season we were determined to try.

On our first two feeds we simply tied off some fish baits and watched what happened. Both times only silvertips took the baits and both times the sharks were very much calmer than any previous experience that we have had with feeding grey reef sharks.

On the following charter we entertained a Japanese friend and Australian diver and film maker Valerie Taylor. Valerie, with her husband Ron, has had more experience filming sharks than anyone else in the world. I was anxious to tell Valerie about our find and to get her expert advice on how to proceed. The advice we received included the news that she knew of only one other reef in the world where silvertip sharks could be found without other sharks being present.

She was very enthusiastic about diving our silvertip reef and explained to us some of the important steps necessary to get very close to the feeding sharks, even hand feed them, without getting bitten. We definitely do not recommend that anyone reading this article attempts to do this, in fact we recommend that you do not.

After a couple more feeds we encouraged the sharks to approach a 'dining area' in a calm and confident manner. Valerie demonstrated that it was possible to hand feed them without causing signs of frenzy. The sharks even showed signs of affection in the same way that a pet dog does. This was rather strange and I have certainly never felt that other sharks, apart from the whale shark, could possibly be friendly. They did not act aggressively to us or to other divers that we brought to the reef.

We now have a situation where, on arriving at the reef, our 'family' is waiting for us. There are at least eight individuals all but one of whom are females, two babies less than one metre long, two adolescents just under two metres long, two adults over two metres long and two grandmothers at nearly three metres, one of which is easily recognised as it has lost half of one of its pectoral fins, presumably to another shark. After we anchor, our guests can see the sharks circling Telita. We give the divers a very detailed briefing then enter with the baits and swim down to the dining area, tying off the dinner to a convenient coral head and keeping a few fish for hand feeding tucked under a plate coral.

The sharks quickly pick up the scent and come in to have their meal. Soon the sharks are swimming around, between and over the divers who can gently touch them as they swim by. A firm tap on the snout is administered if a shark seems to be getting a bit cheeky and this is sufficient to establish control. After each shark has fed from the dining area, Dinah takes a fish in her hand and offers it to one which comes in and sees the bait. After a couple of passes, each time coming a bit closer, seeing and smelling the bait, the shark makes its decision, moves directly to Dinah, closes its eyes and gently takes the bait from her hand. If the bait is moved, it is surprisingly difficult for the shark to find it. Usually the shark will have to make another pass and try again.

We are not trying to tame the sharks and teach them circus stunts, rather to understand them and find ways to communicate with them. We are trying to show the sharks that they can regard us as fellow creatures of the deep, not to fear us, but at the same time to respect us. We are going into their environment, not dragging them into ours. Captive sharks are often dispirited and feeble, in fact many do not survive long in

captivity and bear little relation to the animal in the wild.

These wild sharks have plenty of opportunity to bite divers if they wished. But what we see is a magnificent, glorious creature, perfect in its evolution, and we are happy and grateful to be able to spend a few moments of our lives underwater in awe of the beauty of the beast.

**Top** One of a family of silvertip sharks sweeps past watchful divers. **centre** Silvertips usually approach divers head-on at first sight, swerving away only at the last moment. **bottom** MV Telita at anchor.

# MEN OF
# STATURE

**Left** *A Temboka warrior from the Western Highlands displays his distinctive apron, breastplate and headdress.*

Story and photographs by Kevin Glennon

After a steep climb up into the Bismarck Range on May 26, 1930, two Australian gold prospectors, Michael Leahy and Michael Dwyer, set up camp on the edge of the Eastern Highlands in the then Mandated Territory of New Guinea. As daylight faded, they noticed flickering firelights along the grassy, open valley. They realised that the area they were moving into was heavily populated, not uninhabited as was commonly thought. That the mountainous interior of New Guinea was inhospitable and unpopulated was one of the widely accepted myths among colonial officials and missionaries early this century.

After seven weeks the party reached the south coast of Papua, having traversed one of the main highland valleys and encountered large populations. Driven by the search for gold, Michael Leahy and his brothers spearheaded the exploration of the remaining highland valleys over the next four years.

Today a similar feeling of adventure can be experienced from the comfort of a motor vehicle. The similarities with the early exploratory trips quickly fade as one drives on into the Highlands. The road is a black ribbon flung out along the rolling grasslands and the signposts of Western impact are soon frequent. In the space of 60 years, broad expansive coffee plantations have appeared, and townships with trade stores, markets, airstrips, schools, offices, and residences have been built. But this is all blended in a distinctly PNG way, with Highlands women wearing colorful string bags thronging

**Left** *A mudman from Asaro in the Eastern Highlands with his earthen mask and bamboo claws.* **top right** *Western Highlands women display necklaces of sea shell traded from the coast and cuscus fur headbands.* **bottom right** *Temboka tribesmen from Western Highlands armed with bows and arrows.*

the markets, the slightly ramshackle appearance of trade stores and offices, and a decidedly frontier atmosphere.

The Highlanders of Papua New Guinea are at their most colorful during singsings or festivals held as part of their elaborate ceremonial exchange systems. These are known as moka in the Mount Hagen area, tee in Enga, and mok-ink in parts of the Southern Highlands. It is at these festivals that men demonstrate their wealth by giving it away. The receivers are then placed in debt which they must repay at a later exchange festival. Compensation payments for the death of an enemy tribesman may also be made.

The body decorations consist of bird plumes and feathers; wigs and aprons; animal pelts, furs, bones and insects; cane, bark, leaves, grasses, shells, oils and paints. There is also nowadays the use of plastic beads and powdered paints bought from trade stores as well as an assortment of western objects such as tags, tinsel and drink tops. But bird plumes and feathers remain the main features of body decoration in the Highlands today.

In the Tari region of the Southern Highlands, Huli tribesmen paint their faces a vivid yellow, fashion a crescent-shaped wig from their own hair cuttings, place the iridescent blue breast shield of the superb bird of paradise as a centrepiece of their wig and frame this with red and yellow parrot feathers. On the back of their neck is hung the large beak of a Blythe's hornbill. As a finishing touch they hang tufts of cuscus fur near their temples and crown the lot with

**Top left** *Whole birds and individual feathers make this spectacular headdress.* **bottom left** *Huli wigmen from Southern Highlands with characteristic yellow face adornment.* **right** *Melpa tribesman displays feathers from three species of bird of paradise, human hair wig, cassowary bones, pig tusks, sea shells and croton leaves.* **far right** *A woman from Pangia in Southern Highlands with cane waist bands, bead necklaces and woven headdress.*

the brilliant tail feathers of the Raggiana bird of paradise. The total effect is striking.

Because of the well-noted isolation of the PNG tribes, there is interesting variation in the forms of body decoration within short distances. In the upper Wahgi Valley around Mount Hagen, Melpa tribesmen have their wives or close female relatives make long, sweeping bush string aprons. Across a well oiled chest they hang a crescent of pearl shell and above that is hung bamboo tally sticks. Leaves and grasses are tucked into cane armbands. Faces are painted black, red, yellow and white and at the front of the headnet-covered wig a segment of baler shell is fixed. Not content with this, a headdress is worn consisting of bird of paradise plumage. The crown plumes of the King of Saxony bird of paradise divide a rectangular frame into three sections with feathers of the blue bird of paradise on either side and red parrot feathers in the middle. Crowning the headdress are red tail feathers of the Raggiana bird of paradise. An awesome and impressive sight.

Further variations occur as one travels east down the Wahgi Valley into the Chimbu area and into the Eastern Highlands, then north into the Jimi Valley, or west to the Enga and the Southern Highlands.

With easier communication and travel, it will be interesting to note the degree of homo-genisation that occurs in the body decoration between different tribes. But clan and tribal associations remain strong and with the maintenance of local dialects and languages it is unlikely that customs will change in relation to singsings.

**Top left** *Strings of seeds called Job's tears cover an Eastern Highlander.* **bottom left** *A Western Highlander with a white-painted baler shell head-piece.* **right** *A dancer from Mintima, Simbu, sports long black plumes of the Princess Stephanie bird of paradise, red parrot feathers and a tree kangaroo pelt.*

# Sèpik River

Story and photographs
by Liz Thompson

# CARVINGS

The ancestral wooden carvings of the Sepik River are world famous. Pieces can be found in most major museums and art galleries where they are exhibited as fine examples of tribal art. These carvings have an elusive quality which appeals to people of different cultures. All over the world, the pieces hold a particular charm for those who have no knowledge of their background or original meaning.

The carvings were originally created as part of the animistic way of life practised by the Sepik people. Animism or 'attribution of living soul to inanimate objects' and ancestor worship were chief forms of religious expression before Western missionary contact.

In ancestor worship the individual's or clan's forefathers are immortalised in stories and myths. Ancestors' deeds and exploits are passed down by word-of-mouth across generations who pay homage to them. Spirits of the ancestors are still believed to be present and exercise great power in determining such things as sickness, fertility, productivity of a garden and luck in war. Villagers carve figures in memory of their ancestors, depicting each ancestral spirit's particular image and style. This is to reassure the ancestral spirit that it has not been forgotten and to encourage it to help and protect the carver.

The ancestral figurines have great power. Often kept in the men's 'haus tambaran', they are given offerings of food and betelnut and, as sacred objects, are held in great respect by the villagers.

Sepik masks, as seen in

people of America and Europe. In response to this demand the carvers of the Sepik continue to produce many beautiful pieces.

Using woods such as quila, garamut, cedar and milkwood, the men of the villages Tanbanum, Mindimbit, Yentsuamangua, Koroko, Chambri Lakes and Japanaut busily work with adze and knife. Firstly, they hack out the rough shape of the pieces with an adze. Then the fine work and finishing are completed with the help of a knife made from a heavily ground down bastard file.

Once carved, the piece is 'cooked', or singed black over the fire. This seals the wood and creates a surface texture over which polychrome ochres can be painted. A lined, symmetrical face is painted on with clear representation of tribal patterns and clan markings. Shells are added for eyes and decoration. Final touches include cassowary feathers, shell inlaid putty, feathers, flowers, string tassels, and sometimes a woven cane surround.

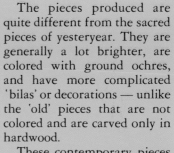

The pieces produced are quite different from the sacred pieces of yesteryear. They are generally a lot brighter, are colored with ground ochres, and have more complicated 'bilas' or decorations — unlike the 'old' pieces that are not colored and are carved only in hardwood.

These contemporary pieces are made with a different objective in mind — to turn the head of an admirer of tribal art rather than to impress an ancestor. However, villagers still show the skill of many generations of fine woodworking experience. Their ability to create expressive pieces out of ochre and wood is still acknowledged worldwide. The fact that these pieces are now displayed more in art galleries and less in museums suggests that there is still great appreciation and fascination for this art form.

**Inset, top** *Maprik Village spirit house decoration.* **centre** *Ceremonial mask serving as a lamp shade.* **bottom** *Blackwater River carvers.*

**Title page** *Tambanum Village carving.*

**Facing page** *Kabriman Village spirit house.* **inset, top** *Mask carver at work.* **inset, bottom** *Garamut drums.*

**This page, top** *Partly completed Tambanum Village mask.* **inset** *Stoking a fire to singe carvings.* **bottom** *Sissano Lagoon, West Sepik.*

many of the world's art galleries, were made for specific ceremonies. Minai masks for example, are usually made as a set of four, including the older brother, older sister, younger brother and younger sister. They are strapped on to large rattan costumes during initiation ceremonies and the wearer takes on the persona of the ancestor. For the skin-cutting ceremony a sacred flute is played and the spiritual presence of the ancestors strengthens the act of initiation regarding manhood and the tribe.

Sabi masks have another purpose. Originally fixed to the centre of a V-shaped bark shield, they were placed in the bow of war canoes during times of conflict. As large canoes full of tribesmen engaged in combat moved across the water and horns were blown, the Sabi mask was the focus of the enemy's gaze. Hung on the front of the canoe, its function was to strike fear and apprehension into the enemy.

Of the many different types of carvings these examples provide only a rough idea of the diversity of pieces produced. Today a wide range of carvings is still made and much of the inspiration to produce them lies in commercial rather than spiritual motivation.

Since the first Germans sailed up the Sepik nearly 100 years ago, the world has been fascinated by the carvings and craftsmen of the river. Collecting expeditions have visited the Sepik regularly since those days and a vast number of pieces has been scattered around the globe. Something about the wooden figures and ochred faces still proves irresistible to the culture-hungry

# B·A·T·T·L·E
## of the
# Coral Sea

Story and photographs by Bruce Hoy

Fifty years ago, Port Moresby was under threat of invasion. Imperial Japanese forces occupied much of the Mandated Territory of New Guinea and seemed unconquerable. They had taken Rabaul and occupied Kieta, Kavieng, Gasmata, Lae and Salamaua. Japanese aerial attacks were being directed against the Allied citadel of Port Moresby, in particular its airfield at Seven Mile, and by May, 1942, the city was under a direct threat of invasion from the sea.

Despite Japan's spectacular achievements in establishing a new empire with strong defensive perimeters, giving it access to badly needed raw materials, there still remained the thorn of the American Pacific Fleet. An urgent need also existed to strengthen and enlarge the defensive perimeter to counter the growing Allied forces in Australia; a need that meant going beyond basic war plans.

Planning for the Port Moresby–Tulagi invasion, code-named Operation MO, began in earnest in early 1942.

The plan was to invade Port Moresby by sea and to meet any challenge from the Allied naval fleet. The capture of Tulagi in the Solomons was an ancillary part of the operation, to protect the eastern flank of the Japanese on New Britain.

With planning completed, the harbors of Rabaul in New Britain and Truk in the Japanese Mandated Territory became a beehive of activity. On April 28,

1,400km to the north of Rabaul at Truk, the Main Support Force comprising four heavy cruisers and the Close Support Force of a light aircraft carrier and a destroyer sailed for southern waters, west of Bougainville.

**Right** *Seen from the floatplane catapault of the cruiser Minneapolis, two destroyers evacuate crew from the Lexington.* **inset** *Deboyne Islands, a Japanese stronghold.*

Next day, two light cruisers, a seaplane tender and three gunboats departed Rabaul to provide additional protection for the invasion force. The Tulagi Invasion Force of two destroyers, three minelayers, one transport and auxiliary craft left Rabaul another day later.

On May 1, the Carrier Strike Force, intended to trap any Allied interference to Operation MO, sailed from Truk. This Force comprised the battle veteran aircraft carriers Shokaku and Zuikaku, both of which had participated in the Pearl Harbor attack and the Rabaul invasion, two heavy cruisers and six destroyers. Three days later, the Port Moresby Invasion Force sailed from the comparative safety of Rabaul. The final chess piece of this complicated manoeuvre was the Attack Force, a light cruiser, five destroyers, one patrol boat and auxiliary craft which departed Rabaul on May 5.

The landings at Tulagi on May 3 were unopposed, the small Australian garrison having withdrawn the previous day. Although the Japanese knew that an American aircraft carrier task force was in the area, the exact composition and its whereabouts were unknown. The Allied forces knew of the pending operation as US Naval Intelligence had already broken the Japanese naval code. The exact plan was unknown, except that it involved a southerly expansion. On May 4, the Japanese at Tulagi suddenly became aware of the presence of an American task force, when 46 aircraft from the USS Yorktown swept in on the Japanese forces unloading, sinking the destroyer Kikuzuki. A second strike at noon sank two patrol boats and damaged an escaping transport, the Tama, which sank several days later.

The Port Moresby invasion fleet having just left the confines of Rabaul Harbor, the American carrier attack at Tulagi meant that the first carrier-versus-carrier battle in naval history was not far off. The Japanese Carrier Strike Force

from Truk was then 400 nautical miles east of Rabaul, sailing in a southeasterly direction. By nightfall on May 5, the fleet had rounded San Cristobal Island and was steering northwest towards the Solomon Sea, and Papua New Guinea waters.

Meanwhile, the Yorktown task force, after its attack on Tulagi, had turned south and joined up with the aircraft carrier USS Lexington and its task force. As the Japanese and American battle groups started groping for each other, the Japanese invasion force, together with its covering ships, steamed towards Port Moresby.

On May 7, a Japanese reconnaissance aircraft came across an American oiler and its covering destroyer, incorrectly identifying them as being an aircraft carrier with a covering cruiser. Both US vessels were repeatedly hit by attack aircraft and sank. This was a costly mistake, for while Japanese aircraft were pounding both vessels, they missed the opportunity of attacking the main American fleet with its carriers. Meanwhile, the Americans had located the Carrier Strike Force from Truk and the Close Support Force from Rabaul.

The American attack started a little after 11am, concentrating on the light carrier Shoho. It put up a valiant fight but was overwhelmed by the 93 attacking aircraft. Three defending fighters were shot down. The Shoho was sunk taking with it 21 aircraft and 638 of its crew. With their carrier beneath the sparkling waters of the Coral Sea, northeast of Misima Island, four remaining Zero fighters headed for the Japanese seaplane base in Deboyne Lagoon, where they were successfully ditched. American losses for the day were three Dauntless dive-bombers and four Wildcat fighters, the fighters during a skirmish against Japanese aircraft from the Shokaku and Zuikaku which in the late afternoon were searching for the American carrier fleet.

Interestingly, one of the Wildcat pilots lost during this action was Ensign Leslie L B Knox, who was born in Brisbane, Australia, and who had gone to the United States, joining the US Navy in April 1939. Knox is believed to be the first Australian killed during the Battle of the Coral Sea.

The next morning, May 8, both opposing forces found

**Above left** Evacuation of the Lexington is completed by whaleboat. **above right** End is near for the burning aircraft carrier.

**Above** Explosions rip the Lexington as it is scuttled by torpedoes from the destroyer Phelps (left).

**Below** Torlesse Islands, a Japanese floatplane base. **inset** Horizontal tailplane from a Mitsubishi 'Pete' floatplane.

each other's carriers; aircraft from the Yorktown and Lexington attacking the two Japanese aircraft carriers. By the time the attack was finished the Shokaku had suffered damage from three bombs that had struck the flight deck and bridge, but the Zuikaku, having slipped beneath cloud cover, was untouched.

Meanwhile, Japanese aircraft attacked the Lexington, scoring numerous bomb hits, as well as torpedo strikes. The Yorktown was not neglected, and although it suffered several bomb hits, it managed to evade the torpedoes aimed at it. By the time the Japanese broke off the attack, the Lexington was being wrecked by internal explosions which resulted in the ship being abandoned. Six hours later, torpedoed by the destroyer Phelps, the Lexington slipped beneath the waves, taking with her 216 men and 36 aircraft. Twenty other American naval aircraft were lost in combat during the day, as against 22 Japanese fighter, torpedo and dive bombers. A further 12 aircraft were jettisoned from the Zuikaku as being too badly damaged, for a total loss of 35.

Early on May 8, with the aircraft carrier Shokaku on its way back to Truk for repairs, the light carrier Shoho sunk, the Invasion and its Supporting

**Above** *Smoke curls from the flight deck of the doomed Lexington.*

Forces milling around to the north of the Trobriand Islands, the Japanese commander in Rabaul, Admiral Inouye, ordered the Invasion Force to return to Rabaul. Several hours later, this order was countermanded by Admiral Isoroku Yamamoto, Commander-in-Chief Combined Fleet, with orders to "annihilate remaining enemy forces".

It took two days to regroup the dispersed Strike and Attack Forces, by which time the American Task Force with the Yorktown was already well south and beyond further contact. On May 11, the Japanese Carrier Strike Force was ordered to return to Truk.

The first naval battle fought solely by aircraft was over. At no stage was there any ship-to-ship engagement nor any account by any sailor on either side of having sighted an enemy vessel.

Port Moresby was safe from an invader for the time being, but would soon come under the threat of another invasion, this time by land.

**Left** *Lexington flight deck during the battle.*

# Garden of EDEN

**Below** *Giant vase sponge on Sheila's Reef.* **far right** *Part of Salamaua's peninsula, seen from the headland.* **inset** *Spectacularly colored anemone fish are also* ~~known as clown fish~~

Story and photographs by Tony Karacsonyi

Background *Salamaua's peninsula.* **left** *Gorgonia fans at Halfway Reef.* **top right** *Salamauan girls pause on the way home from school.* **centre right** *Pink tubular sponges on Sheila's Reef.* **bottom right** *MV Barbarian.*

I magine an undersea pinnacle rising from the depths to within 26 metres of the ocean's surface, the peak a Garden of Eden of marine life, some of it of gigantic proportions.

The place exists and is known as Halfway Reef, lying halfway between Lae and Salamaua in the Huon Gulf on the north coast of Papua New Guinea. It was discovered accidentally by Rod Pearce, the owner-skipper of the diving charter vessel Barbarian and proprietor of the Salamaua Divers Lodge.

As we descended, the top few metres of water were murky due to river runoff. Suddenly the water changed to a clear inky blue and we beheld a breathtaking scene. Tan and purple soft corals stood two metres high, like trees in a forest, while others, riddled with featherstars, spread horizontally across the reef. To touch the bottom here is to touch living things, as the entire peak is covered in rich green algae, soft and hard corals. A mammoth basket sponge towered almost three metres high and one-and-a-half metres in diameter. As Linda Kavanagh stood beside the sponge on her fin tips the sponge still towered above her. Had she taken off her tank she could easily have fitted inside.

From this remarkable sponge, Rod led us over Halfway's sheer walls to see the 'hanging gardens' at 39 metres. These gardens of gorgonia fans dribbling from the overhangs had the grandeur of the Hanging Gardens of Babylon.

It is hard to believe that Salamaua was once the scene of fierce warfare between Japanese and Allied forces during World War II. The area was captured by the Japanese in 1942 later to be reclaimed by Allied troops, with heavy losses on both sides. The jungle has now hidden many of the war's scars but several anti-aircraft guns remain on Salamaua's headland, one near the school house and the other in the heart of the local village.

Salamaua is an ideal destination for novice divers. Rod and Linda carefully lead them so that by the end of their stay they are confidently diving to 40 metres.

Sheila's Reef was one of our first dives, where Rod could assess individual abilities. Little did we know this was a world class reef. The plateau at 21 metres was covered in beds of whip gorgonia in full white polyp bloom, gorgonia fans, large delicate vase sponges, all of which were heavily laden in crinoids. Purple soft corals leaned like streamers in the current and elegant fairy basslets hovered over a coral head, creating a beautiful scene.

We later dived Sheila's Reef to 36 metres specifically to photograph a single gorgonia fan whose dimensions were staggering. At four metres long and two metres high it was the largest one my dive buddy, Heather, and I had ever seen. Its lip was laden with crinoids and curled over slightly with the current like a huge orange wave. Heather swam into its curl where her entire body length was framed.

There are many other spectacular sites in the area including Georgia's Pinnacle, with some large growth and pelagic fish species but lacking the absolute splendor of Halfway Reef. Sheperton Shoals is a reef plateau and a melting pot of fish species including some large silver trevally. The Beacon, another site, was sheltered and close to the lodge. We found it to be a photographer's paradise with plenty of hard coral, black coral bushes, and anemones with commensal shrimps at depths of one metre to 25 metres.

**Above** *A leisurely decompression stop at Sheperton Shoals.* **right** *Ron Pearce, host and dive guide, doubles as barbecue chef.* **top right** *Soft corals at Halfway Reef.* **bottom right** *Vivid butterfly cod at Georgia's Pinnacle.*

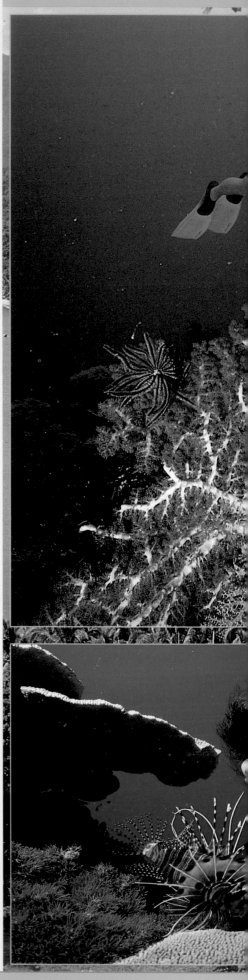

Snorkelling just outside the lodge was also fascinating. Here we found black diadema urchins with electric blue markings. Swimming vertically among one of the urchin's spines was a razor fish. Its transparent body with black stripe was a perfect camouflage.

Dolphins can often be seen from the verandah of the lodge porpoising in the shimmer of the flat sea and orcas inhabit the waters about Salamaua during April and May.

Salamaua impressed us with its raw beauty; its steep mountainous shores draped in green jungle falling into the still ocean to be met by hard coral reefs, frigate birds soaring high in the sky; the drone of cicadas through the hot humid days and birds calling from coconut palms. Salamaua is the doorstep to some of the world's great diving sites.

Air Niugini operates regular services between Port Moresby and Lae.

Dive Adventures Australia arrange diving holidays to the Salamaua Divers Lodge.

**Right** *Part of Salamaua's peninsula.* **below** *Flowering seawhips.*

# Striking it rich in Bulolo

Story by Michael Gebicki

Bulolo, which once attracted eager travellers in search of gold, has struck it rich again with a new source of temptation for those wanting a life of comfort. Although open since the 1950s, Pine Lodge bears little resemblance to its former self. The same company that busily dredged the Bulolo Valley for gold also built Pine Lodge but allowed it to deteriorate badly after dredging ended in the mid-sixties. When manager, Brian Riches arrived four years ago, the garden shade had run riot,

## Photographs by Michael Gebicki and Wendy Stone

roofs leaked and the dining room fly-wire was peeling from the window frames. Brian remembers one night when a guest's bed fell through the rotted floorboards.

Recently the lodge was bought by Melanesian Tourist Services who wrought many changes.

Set on a ridge above the township of Bulolo, Pine Lodge now has two rows of neat green wooden bunga-lows, each divided into two units, separated by an avenue of flame-of-the-forest trees. It is probably the only hotel in the world with an aviary outside each room, filled with colorful eclectus parrots or fabulous birds of paradise.

Each of Pine Lodge's 14 spacious units is comfortably furnished with a single as well as queen sized bed, an ensuite bathroom, refrigerator, tea and coffee-making facilities and overhead fan. A sliding picture window opens on a large balcony with views across the cool, moist land-scape of the Bulolo Valley. At almost 1,000 metres, the air is a welcome relief from the clammy heat of the coast – invigorating but still warm enough for an early morning dip in the lodge's pool.

Days at Pine Lodge are spent in four-wheel-drive vehicles, in the care of knowledgeable local guides, exploring the misty mountain valleys and secluded villages of the area. This is not the Papua

Wendy Stone

Wendy Stone

83

New Guinea of plumed tribesmen and full-blooded singsings, but the diversity of its tribal cultures, scenery, history, bird and insect life makes a visit to Bulolo an important part of any traveller's itinerary.

Bulolo is located in Morobe Province, one of the last areas of PNG to be opened to the outside world. The upland valleys of this region were the home of the fierce Kukukuku tribesmen, the short, stocky warriors whose lightning raids spread terror through the lowland villages. It was only when gold was discovered along the Bulolo and the Upper Watut Valleys in the 1920s that the first white men came, followed by government patrol officers bringing semblance of order.

The first prospectors to arrive and survive the arrows of the Kukukuku made legendary fortunes. Along some parts of Edie Creek, a cubic yard of river gravel yielded 50 ounces of gold – worth about 15,000 kina at today's prices. But the greatest fortune was extracted by the gold dredges, the clanking mechanical juggernauts that scooped the gold from 20 metres below the surface. By 1939 there were eight 2,000-tonne dredges at work around Bulolo, every part air-lifted into the area and assembled, in one of the most imaginative feats of engineering.

The dredges finished their work 20 years ago. Two are located a short distance from Pine Lodge. These giant rusting dinosaurs are being slowly reclaimed by the jungle. Gold is still mined upstream from Bulolo, along the road to Wau, mostly by simple sluices and panning. Anyone can try their hand with a borrowed pan, although the proceeds cannot be kept.

Even if they don't strike it rich, visitors can hardly fail to enjoy the scenery. Early one morning we followed the Bulolo River downstream

**Facing page** *Open air cemeteries contain ancient smoked bodies and skeletal remains.* **This page, left** *Children from a Watut Valley village.* **above** *Bulolo market scenes.*

toward Lae, then turned off where the Snake River cuts through the hills. For almost an hour we travelled along its banks, on a rocky road winding through the bottom of a spectacularly steep valley glazed with the deep green velvet of kunai grass, past silver waterfalls that fell in a glistening arc from the high slopes. Eventually the river narrowed and we surged across and on to a rutted track that led to the village of Mapos.

In the company of a village elder and a dozen excited children, we worked our way for 20 minutes down the hillside and fell into the cool, rushing water at the bottom. The cliffs along this section of the river are pitted with deep limestone caves, some of which were once used as local burial grounds. Open air burials are now a thing of the past, but skeletal remains can still be seen clearly on rock ledges above the river. The adjacent cliffs have been daubed with ochre stick figures that bear a curious resemblance to the rock paintings of the Australian Aborigines.

These Highlands river valleys are home to one of the largest and most exotic insect populations on earth: butterflies. They are everywhere – dancing through the undergrowth on iridescent blue wings, fluttering along the shaded riverbanks, even dive bombing the swimming pool at Pine Lodge. Bulolo is the site of the Insect Farm and Trading Agency, a government organisation that links butterfly collectors and farmers in PNG with buyers around the world. Many butterflies are found only here, such as the king of the butterfly world, Ornithoptera alexandrae. A visit to the agency's headquarters is worthwhile, to see where the butterflies are hatched and exhibited under glass as well as prepared for export.

No trip to Pine Lodge is complete without a visit to Kukukuku country. The tribes

Wendy Stone

in this region now refer to themselves by other names – Watut or Menye, for example – but they still live much as they always have, farming sweet potatoes and hunting birds with the powerful black palm bows that once sent shivers down their neighbors' spines.

The dirt road from Bulolo to Menyamaya, the main town of Kukukuku country, was carved out of the rainforests almost a decade ago. The long, tortuous drive crosses the green slopes of the Watut valley and climbs into the clouds. For almost

**Top** Pine Lodge bungalow. **centre left** Watut Valley. **centre right** Pine Lodge swimming pool. **bottom** Shallow but delightful hot springs, Bulolo.

Wendy Stone

Wendy Stone

**Top** *Gold dredge near Bulolo.* **centre left** *Kukukuku man in traditional dress.* **centre right** *Fun in the Snake River.* **bottom** *Young villager rugs up against the cool mountain mist.*

three hours we bumped along the road, charging across rivers on wooden bridges and squeezing past the landslides that nearly blocked our passage. Rain fell constantly in a fine spray that sparkled in tiny jewelled droplets on the moss that covered everything. Now and again we passed thatched houses huddled together in a clearing where the village children shouted and waved to us. Sometimes we saw a family walking along the road and sheltered by hooded bark capes.

At Aseki, almost 100 kilometres from Bulolo, we stopped at a trail leading up to a steep hillside. Slipping and sliding on the muddy track, we climbed through dripping ferns, clambering over the roots of giant pandanus palms that blocked out the light, to arrive at the shelter of a steep cliff face to see a row of six ochre colored bodies, frighteningly well-preserved. Traditionally the people of this area smoked the bodies of their dead, a method which allowed them to keep watch over their former territory. The old burial sites are still maintained.

It was late afternoon when we emerged from the clouds and into the clear, sunny skies around Bulolo. As a final treat to finish off a hard day, Ken, our guide and driver from Pine Lodge, took us to a hot water creek where we soaked in the warm, soothing water, listening to the forest birds singing their evening operetta, with the sunlight spilling through the bamboo stalks in long, molten shafts.

No more gold in the Bulolo Valley? Don't you believe it.

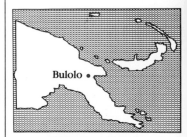

Air Niugini operates daily services linking Lae with Port Moresby and other centres.

Bulolo can be reached by road or light aircraft from Lae.

Story and photographs
by Keith Briggs

# TREE OF LIFE

The sago tree provides more of the essentials of life for village people than any other single tree in the bush. Although looked upon primarily as a source of food, during the 15 to 20 years it takes to mature to the stage where it can be processed into sago flour, it contributes many of life's necessities.

**Left** *Mature sago tree.*

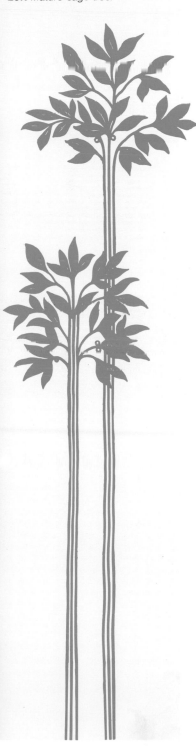

**Inset above** *Paring sago pith.* **top**
*Sago making trough.*
**bottom** *House with sago thatch
roof and plaited sago frond walls.*

As a young tree, even before a definite trunk forms and while it is still a maze of spiky fronds or limbs, the leaves are selectively pruned for use as roofing material for dwellings. Apart from the Nipa palm on the coast, there is no substitute for sago thatch on the lowlands. At higher altitudes kunai grass provides the roofing. House gables are usually closed in with sago leaf that is first fixed to thin sticks and then held in place with cane binding.

The lower limbs of the sago die off as the trunk grows. These are fairly straight and are cut to form vertical outer cladding for house walls. If cut while green the hard shiny skin is peeled off in long thin strips and plaited into a pleasantly patterned wall lining or floor covering inside the house. Our house in Tari has two walls in each of six rooms lined with this attractive material.

Boys use the ribs of the leaves as toy arrows with a small square of leaf left at the end as a 'feather' or flight.

People working in the swamps invariably get a thorn or two in their feet, so two hard, dry sago leaf spines are used as needles to remove the offending piece from the tough sole.

When the new leaves are unfolding from their sheaths they are stripped and twisted into a fine string by rolling on the thigh in the same way as bilum (carry bag) twine is made. The outstanding skirts worn by married women are made from this string. At this same stage the new, almost white, filmy fronds are often

**Inset** *Sago grubs.* **above**
*Celebrating a successful sago harvest.*

used as bunting to decorate a new church, classroom or aid post or to line the path down to the river where baptisms will take place. From this too, men make the spectacular waterfall effect and the small skirts they wear as part of their elaborate dancing regalia.

Boys make toy aircraft from the balsawood-like pith of the limbs.

Thin sheets cut from the edges of the frond butts are made into dishes and tubs, the most common being those in which the bright red pandanus

sauce is prepared. They are very durable and the dogs always lick them nice and clean after use! The flat, wide frond butts make excellent sleds for the children, which bigger boys pull down steep slopes at high speed.

When the sago reaches maturity and the seed bearing antlers appear at the top, the tree is felled for the sago making process. Two large limbs are prised off and their butts joined to form a trough supported by forked sticks and other framework. The hard

bark is laid back from the trunk and the women sit and pare or shave off the pith with deft and powerful strokes of their sago adzes fitted with sharp edged stone bits mounted in black palm handles. The resultant coarse sawdust-like material is beaten and washed in the trough to separate the fine white powder which is carried down by the water into bark tubs.

The damp flour is packed into large tubular containers made from sago leaves, pinned together with short pieces of

**Above** *Kaukau and wild sugar cane supplement the sago diet.* **top right** *Skirt made from sago leaf.* **bottom right** *Sago flour going into a leaf, to be tied and cooked.*

leaf rib. The sago flour is the staple diet of most people in Papua New Guinea who live at altitudes below about 650 metres. The innumerable ways in which sago can be cooked would fill a book, but one common method is to make a long parcel of flour in a sago leaf and cook it over a low fire.

Another edible portion of the tree is obtained from in the crown where the top branches join. The head and top section of the trunk are left for large black beetles to lay their eggs. These develop into the plump fatty grubs so prized as a

delicacy. As the grubs mature the men enclose the tree head in a high fence of sapling stakes securely bound with cane. A portcullis type trapdoor of hard, heavy sago tree bark is suspended in the narrow door way with a trigger set at a suitable point within the enclosure. Wild pigs who smell the grubs and come in to enjoy a feast trip the trigger and are trapped inside to become a feast themselves.

Once the pigs have been given the chance to be caught, the last thing the tree does is to give its harvest of grubs as

the whole rotting head is broken up with axes and knives in the search for them.

Nothing is wasted, so all that remains is an abandoned trough and the long slabs of bark where the tree lay to give up its life-giving sustenance.

It is not a tree that features on calendar pictures or travel brochures, framing sunsets and blue bays as does the coconut. Hardly seen in its swampy home, unheard of and unsung by the outside world nevertheless throughout its life and in its death it serves mankind well.

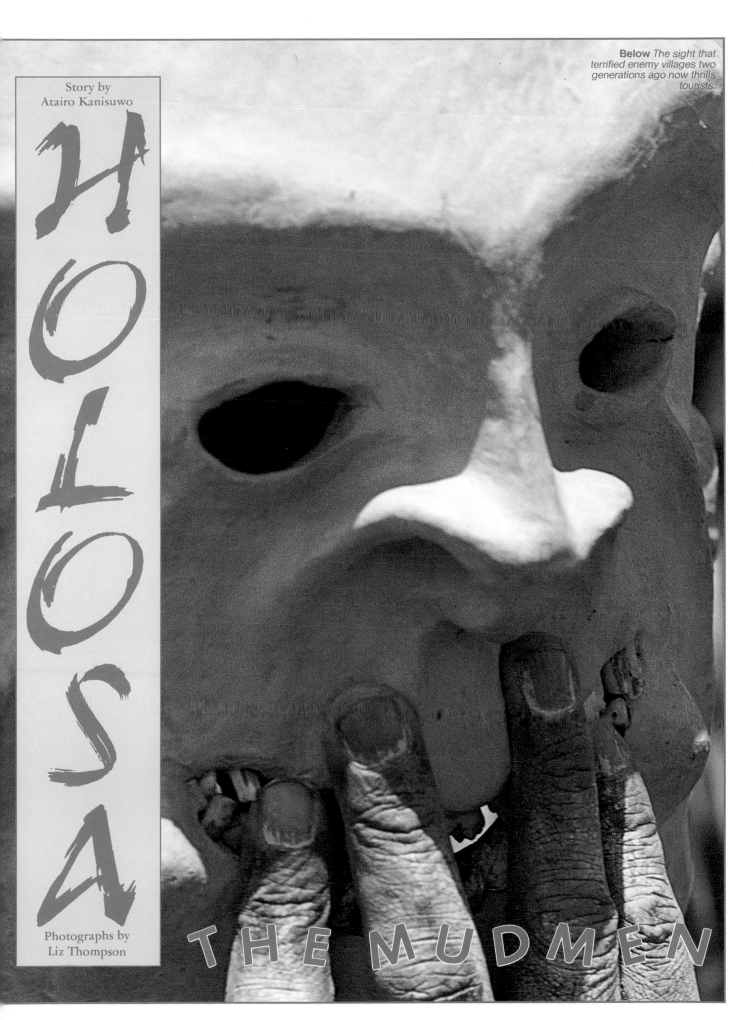

# HOLOSA

Story by
Atairo Kanisuwo

Photographs by
Liz Thompson

## THE MUDMEN

Now that the Asaro mudmen have become one of Papua New Guinea's premier tourist attractions, I will tell you my small history about how they came to be.

I heard this story from my father. The 'holosa', as the mudmen used to be called in my mother tongue, were started by my grandfather, Pukiro Pode. Originally the mudmen, the holosa, came from Komunive village in the Asaro Valley. There are four clans within the village, but the mudmen originated from my clan, Gavina. The other clans are Sehayuha, Okorohayuha and Ganadiyuha.

**Facing page, top** *Mudmen donning their masks for a show.* **facing page, lower** *Mudmen at the Goroka Show.* **left** *Resting after the exertions of a mudmen's dance.*

During those primitive times, tribal wars between villages were common and severe. In order to live, villagers battled each other for land which, of course, is a big thing. The champion village then looted off everything wherever they found it. Their loots were usually pigs, crops, women and children, but usually male children were killed.

Then there came a time when two brothers, my grandfather, Pukine Pode and Tupunuluva Pode, created something new to help in fights against other villages. They explained their plan and suggestions with their clan men who accepted them. The next day, the whole village knew the plan and knew that the two men's suggestions would work out right and a whole mob headed towards a nearby enemy village, which was Kenetisaro.

The plan, of course, was for my grandfather and his brother to be holosa and terrify the enemy.

When people in the village saw the first mudmen, they fled in all directions leaving their belongings behind.

Truly, it was the very first sight in their lives of such horrific figures coming towards their village. Thereon, my grandfather and the men started shooting arrows at their enemies, killing all men and leaving almost an emptied village. The idea had really worked and truly it was a big success. So for years my ancestors used such ways of terrorising their enemies and killing them.

The first mudmen used the 'gotaraha', which in my mother tongue is a garment, usually shaped with eyes, nose and a mouth. My grandfather and his brother coated theirs with white mud all over the head and the body.

When it came to my father's age, the way of dressing had a slight change. He and other holosa made masks out of raw bamboo which could be just fitted over the head. The bamboo frame was then coated with white mud.

**Top** Pig tusks decorate one mask (left), another (right) is modelled after a human skull. **above** A mudman mask with a pig-like face.

Nowadays we use permanent masks made of pure white or a gray mud. The masks can be 1 to 2cm thick and carefully shaped like big bowls. The nose and the ears are made separately and fitted on to the masks while holes are made for the eyes and the mouth. The teeth are usually pigs' teeth and tusks. Others prefer to use human teeth or cuscus teeth.

When you look at mudmen, what a sight it is. Sometimes you can never tell at all whether it is a human figure or a beast.

Some time ago, my fellow mudmen and I made several tours overseas. Our first tour was in America in 1978 and twice in Australia in 1979 and 1980. Back in PNG we also made several tours to other provinces to perform on big occasions such as the opening of a new building.

I am very proud of our culture and tradition as a whole. Therefore we have to remind our youngsters always to preserve our culture and traditions. We are planning ahead to boost our mudmen attraction to many more people, especially our tourists who might have heard of the mudmen but who have had no chance to see the reality.

With my final words I want to say that I like the name 'holosa' as it used to be. But we appreciate the name, mudmen, and that is now our registered name.

**Top** *The modern face of a mudman's mask, with the hint of a smile.* **right** *By contrast, a mask with glowering, threatening features.*

I recently returned to Wuvulu Island after an absence of more than a decade. This time around, my aim was to film killer whales in clear water. Although we had filmed orcas elsewhere, conditions had always been difficult because the water visibility was limited or the whales were shy. Excerpts below from my personal journal tell what followed.

It is raining. We decide to explore a cave. In the vicinity of the cave three orcas appear, one a male.

As he approaches, I notice something strange about the shape of his mouth. I wonder if it is damaged or has been injured. We attempt to approach but the orca is not interested.

# encounter with
# ORCAS

Story and Photographs by Jean-Michael Cousteau

Soon though, it passes by us and we are shocked! We are witnessing something probably never before seen by humans. We are in the middle of a hunt. The orca has a two-metre manta ray in its mouth!

We hang suspended in the blue, transfixed as the orca shakes its victim. Flesh is torn, pieces drift toward the depths, blood expands in a murky cloud. The carcass has great chunks missing and begins to sink. Suddenly the orca swoops down and retrieves its prey. The shaking begins again and eventually most of the manta is consumed. Bits and pieces drift off in the current to nourish others in the food web.

Next day, we follow the orcas one-and-one half times around Wuvulu Island as we witness more remarkable events.

Around midday the orcas cease all swimming and hang head down, suspended at about 45 degrees angle. They rise to the surface to breathe every few minutes. To us the impression is that of a siesta.

About an hour later the male descends out of sight, returns, and swims directly in front of us as if to show off what it is holding. A two-metre shark limply struggles in its grip. Moments later a female emerges from the depths also with a shark in her mouth. The orcas parade past, giving us the impression that they are showing off their catch.

**Above** Killer whale (orca) surfaces near Wuvulu Island.
**Left** Orca eating a shark.
**Right** Resting after the feast.

# SEED HUNTERS

Story by Ingrid Strewe
Photographs by Oliver Strewe

Tree Seed Centre scientists from Canberra have made two expeditions in the past two years into the hot humid Oriomo Plateau region in Western Province, Papua New Guinea, collecting seed from several trees, in particular Acacia mangium. Known in Australia as a fairly scrubby little tree the Acacia mangium grows straight and tall in PNG.

**Left** *Seed hunter, Brian Gunn, pressing a flower in the field.* **inset** *Typical tropical tree seed pod.*

Last year, Maurice McDonald and Brian Gunn flew into Daru, the provincial capital and administrative centre of the Western Province of PNG, for their second visit in two years. They had with them enough equipment to make an independent expedition into Western Province, including 4,000 rounds of ammunition for two rifles, used to shoot down seed-laden branches.

McDonald and Gunn hired three boats in Daru to take them up the Oriomo River to the area where they intended to concentrate their collections. Demand for seed from this area is particularly high because of its superior growth rates.

They were fortunate to find very large crops and engaged the local villagers to make extensive seed collections.

Some had done the work before during the previous expedition. All were good collectors as they knew the tree species well.

The acacia species are in high demand for pulp, reafforestation after shifting cultivation and soil stabilisation following logging in rain forest. Requests for seed from PNG is particularly high and is increasing. There is rising

**Left** *Oriomo Plateau villagers bring in seed pods for drying.*

demand from countries in the wet humid tropics as acacias' natural role is as secondary forest growth. Disturbed or destroyed forest must pass through several stages, gradually returning to rainforest condition. The rapidly growing acacia shades out the useless bladey imperata grass, enriches the soil (fixing nitrogen) and nurses other rain forest species as they recolonise sites. In some sterile areas of Thailand, Malaysia, Laos, the Philippines and Vietnam these species offer the only hope of ensuring a continuing supply of high quality timber and aiding rainforest regrowth.

Arid zones such as West Africa have different problems that are being overcome by the same species. Here there is a heavy human and animal pressure on the landscape and although the native acacias are useful they are slow growing and are no longer coping with demand. Australian and PNG species, already popular in places like Senegal and the

**Clockwise, from top** *Acacia seed pods; Brian Gunn cleaning seeds with villagers; acacia flowers; Oriomo Plateau landscape.*

Cape Verde Islands, are being planted as protection around native species. Then when fuel wood is needed the nomadic herdspeople are more likely to cut down an Australian acacia than the slow-growing local which is the better fodder tree for their herds.

The United Nations' Food and Agriculture Organisation estimates that almost one third of the world's population depends solely on wood for cooking and heating. In developing countries a massive 86 per cent of the annual consumption of wood is used for fuel and the FAO has forecast a deficit of more than 100 million hectares of plantation by the year 2000.

**Right** *Pigeon hunter Nike Nike takes aim (tree marked for preservation).* **below** *Acacia mangium seed.*

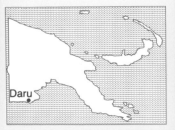

**Left** *Brian Gunn buying seed from collectors.*

# CREATING A
# WINNER

Story and photographs by Lyn and Pat Manly

**Below** *Max Benjamin developed palm oil plantation and dive resort.*

**Centre** *Comfortable guest bungalow at Walindi.* **bottom** *Beautiful feather starfish,*

**Top & bottom** *Coral comes in many shapes and colors.* **centre** *Kimbe Bay angel fish.*

Walindi Plantation Diving Resort, near Kimbe in the West New Britain Province of Papua New Guinea, is a favorite of divers from all over the world. In October 1989 Walindi was deservedly honored (with two other international resorts) when voted as offering the 'best reef diving from a resort' outside the Caribbean, by members of In Depth, an independent journal published in the United States.

Walindi started in 1969 when an Australian agriculturalist, Max Benjamin, bought a broken-down cocoa plantation. He first came to PNG in 1966, a Diploma in Agriculture filed in his briefcase. Working for the Department of Agriculture, Stock and Fisheries under the Australian administration meant a steady salary, most of which he saved towards enrolment fees at Aberdeen College in Scotland. The grand plan was to fulfil a long-time ambition to study cattle breeding and genetics.

This particular ambition was never realised. He did not anticipate the effect the Kimbe area of New Britain would have on him. His government work saw him engaged as an Agricultural Officer working on the Hoskins Oil Palm Project, the pioneer oil palm development in PNG. It was found that the region was endowed with a humid climate and an average annual rainfall of 380mm that could irrigate the rich volcanic, pumice-based soil. That, coupled with a lack of cyclones or strong winds, meant the region was ideal for oil palm cultivation.

By 1970 Max was truly settled in West New Britain. He had resigned his government position and was firmly involved in Walindi and the changeover in plantation crops from cocoa to oil palm. Scotland and Aberdeen College were getting further and further away. One dream was fading, others were taking its place.

Acquiring Walindi was the first to permanency in the Kimbe district, the second step was meeting an Australian

agriculturalist, Cecilie Kemp who became his wife and business partner, and mother of their two children. Palm oil from the Kimbe district finds its way around the world for use in margarine, as an ingredient in soap, or as a component of commercial cooking oil.

I asked Max Benjamin if his plans in the early days had included a resort. "No, I didn't give it any thought until late in 1978," he said. "We learned to dive in the mid-seventies and spent our weekends diving and exploring the reefs and pinnacles in Kimbe Bay. Cecilie and I took a vacation to the Red Sea and dived from Israel and discovered that we had better diving right on our doorstep in PNG. I became a dive instructor that same year and taught many of our friends to dive. We used Walindi as a meeting place on weekends. The dive service grew to include a couple of small aluminium runabouts, some scuba cylinders and a small compressor. The operation was very low key, in fact I could not stir up any interest from outside the country."

*Author Lyn Manly in ite environment.* **top right** *ie Benjamin buys uce outside her kitchen* **centre right** *Walindi's ming pool.* **lower right** *e Bay children enjoy ing visitors.*

The progression to a professional resort and dive facility began in 1984 when Walindi gained its first guest bungalows. About the same time, several wholesale travel agents from Sydney visited the area on a fact finding tour. The next year Walindi Plantation Diving Resort was in full swing and started to become known in the Australian marketplace and beyond.

On numerous trips to Walindi we have seen both the resort and the dive operation make steady progress. The resort now has six self-contained bungalows each with private bathroom, as well as four single rooms in the newly renovated original plantation house. All have wonderful views of Kimbe Bay. Sunrise is always something special and well worth catching as slivers of gold and orange light creep across the bay.

Every weekend Max Benjamin can be found out on the dive boat, enjoying his favorite pastime — diving! He shares the divemaster duties with the resident instructor and leads guests on dive tours over some of his favorite sites. "I really want visiting divers to have a good time at Walindi. I have swum with guests among killer whales in the bay. A similar experience occurred with a herd of humpback whales and we regularly spot pilot whales and dugong from the boat. I love swimming with sharks, especially the large school of hammerheads that are occasionally sighted at North Ema Reef. We can give guests the opportunity to see dolphins underwater. Ropes are slung from the dive

Above Kimbe Bay reefs are ideal for snorkelling. **left** On Rainbow Reef.

boat, with two or three snorkellers on each side and we motor at a very slow speed into the pod of dolphins. This has been happening now for about two years, just about every day, so the dolphins are becoming quite used to the boat. They swim just under the surface, only a few metres from the snorkellers and often dart across and back and then leap out of the water".

**Above** Feather starfish are unlikely looking animals.

Reservations for Walindi Plantation Diving Resort can be made through South Pacific Tours, Port Moresby. Phone: 213 500; and Sea New Guinea, 100 Clarence Street, Sydney, NSW 2000. Phone: (02) 267 5563.

Diving from Walindi is always full of surprises. Kimbe Bay is endowed with massive reef systems rising from a deep sea floor. These pinnacles taper off just a few metres under the surface and are laden with a superb array of sedentary growths; thick glades of crimson fire whips and trees of delicate soft corals intermingled among forests of multi-colored sea fans, black corals and sponges. A dive onto one of the Kimbe Bay reefs is like an excursion to an underwater botanical garden. Plants and flowers are replaced by masses of rainbow-hued corals and sponges, the birds and butterflies are represented by exquisite tropical fishes. Each one appears as if handpainted with only the brightest colors from the artist's paintbox.

Max Benjamin is always taking us on tours of discovery; and leading divers onto new reefs, enabling them to have adventures and new experiences. "I get inspired when guests have a really good time at Walindi, it gives me a buzz," he says. "When they book a return holiday then I know that the hard work has all been worthwhile."

Air Niugini operates regular services to Hoskins near Kimbe Bay.

**Above** Rewards for scuba divers are diverse and wonderful sights.

Kimbe Bay

A s explorers who have travelled the planet during the last few decades, my father Jacques Cousteau and I, along with our teams, have come to appreciate the value of cultural practices which connect people to their environment. It has become clear to us that people whose traditions teach them to respect nature are more likely to protect and sustain natural resources than those who have lost their traditional customs. With this in mind, we set out to document on film people who traditionally 'call sharks'.

# SHARK calling

Story and photographs by
Jean-Michael Cousteau and
R.C. Murphy

Our first trip was to the Tabar Islands north of New Ireland, Papua New Guinea. A boat was hired and a search from coastal village to village began. After two days, we met an elderly man who assured us that he could call sharks. Further probing revealed that he had not performed the ritual in 20 years and it would take him at least a month for spiritual and physical preparations. During this conversation, we were surrounded by a crowd of curious young people and we asked the old shark caller if he had a protege. He said that none of the young men were interested in learning the shark-calling ritual. We left saddened by what was probably the death of this tradition in the Tabar Islands.

Our quest next focused on the village of Kontu on the south side of New Ireland. With guidance from the Provincial Government, we had an audience with the Council of Kontu and received permission to film shark caller Selam Karasibe at work, assisted by his protege, Randal.

The process began when Selam dragged his boat to the water's edge and equipped it with traditional rattles made from coconut shells, a spear, a triton shell horn, cigarettes and some coral stones. Out on the water, during a hot day, Selam observed various rituals by dropping the stones, shaking the rattles and chanting. No shark responded. For five frustrating days the process was repeated without result.

Our filming permit was about to expire and I decided that at the end of the seventh day, our ship Alcyone would have to leave Kontu so as to depart PNG on time. Just one hour before the scheduled departure, a shark appeared.

Depending on one's perspective, either the shark spirits responded to the calling or the acoustic sense of the shark directed it to the sounds of the rattles. Either way, the shark approached Selam's boat and began to circle. As it swam

**Right** Shark caller Selam Karasibe signals ...

107

closer, a small fish at the end of a stick was offered. The shark took the bait and made a second pass. Selam lowered a vine noose attached to a piece of wood carved in the shape of a propeller. The shark entered the 'lasso' and Selam gave a mighty pull.

Then battle erupted! The shark struggled with all its might in its own medium of water while above, Selam struggled in the boat. The fight was neither short nor easy.

Above and below-water cinematographers, a still photographer and a sound man, after seven days of waiting, scrambled to capture the drama of the moment. Selam wrestled the shark, lifted it slightly above the water and began to club it into submission. Moments later the shark was hauled aboard. After a cigarette Selam used the triton to signal the village a few miles away that a shark had been called and captured.

This act affirmed the relation-

ship between shark spirit and shark caller since it is believed that the shark voluntarily submits to the caller according to his power. Through the shark caller, who is of a traditional lineage of callers, the entire community is reconnected to the shark spirits and to the natural world. From our perspective, this bonding between man and nature has significant long-term, ecological benefits by fostering respect for other living things. It is our hope that present and future generations will consider such long-standing culture and traditions of sufficient value to preserve.

# ERUPTION below

Story and photographs by
Bob Halstead

Volcanoes in Papua New Guinea are fond of erupting. They also like to growl and threaten and smoke and flare up and generally carry on like spoilt teenagers, which, in terms of the Earth's lifetime, they may well be. I have always been wary of the terms 'dormant' and 'extinct' volcanoes. If it looks like a volcano, watch out for trouble, and if there are several grouped together — well, would you ever trust a group of teenagers not to get up to mischief?

So I was not too surprised when I found out that the 'extinct' volcano called Dobu Island, between Normanby and Fergusson Islands in Milne Bay Province, had an underwater vent that was still active. We knew of the hot springs a few miles away at Kedidia on Fergusson Island, which have geysers and bubbling mud pools, but this was the first time that we had heard of an underwater vent.

It is a strange sight. On one hand you imagine the turmoil beneath the sea bed causing the venting of the gas, one the other you witness an idyllic reef scene

with corals, sea grasses, fishes, sea stars and anemones. All the usual residents of our underwater world are diffused through a curtain of bubbles emerging from the bottom.

In some places a mist of fine bubbles fogs the view, in others large vents belch great balloons of gas which break up and bob their way to the surface.

The gas, presumably from its hydrogen sulphide content, has a foul smell. Because of this, even though the vents are in shallow water, we prefer to use scuba gear and breathe the fresh air from our tanks rather than snorkel. Even so we did not escape totally the effects of the

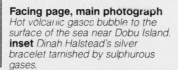

**Facing page, main photograph**
*Hot volcanic gases bubble to the surface of the sea near Dobu Island.* **inset** *Dinah Halstead's silver bracelet tarnished by sulphurous gases.*

gas. My wife Dinah emerged from the water dismayed because her favorite silver heart bracelet, a Valentine's gift from me, had turned black! Fortunately a few weeks swimming in clean ocean restored its natural color.

We expected to see a barren and dead reef surrounding the vents but this was not so. In fact the sea grasses seemed to thrive and were as rich as I have ever seen. Although the biggest vents bleached the rock around their bases, smaller vents were seen emerging right through living reef. Fish and other marine creatures seemed unaffected.

We returned to the vents

**Left** Marine plants grow right to the edge of geothermal vents. **above** Coral on top of a vent. **below** Peaceful Dobu Island gives no clues to the volcanic cauldron below.

later and with clear water about I took some photos. Some divers even made a night dive and reported excellent sightings of molluscs and lion fish. We returned again in November and December. Each time the water was dirty and I was at a loss to explain why since there had not been any recent heavy rain. Our divers entered the water and examined the vents but returned with uneasy feelings and reports of patches of very warm water and strange vibrations. Ian Chapman, a diving instructor and former resident of PNG who now works with the Cousteau Society, decided to try a night dive but he returned after 15 minutes not at all happy with the experience. He could not describe exactly what the matter was but said he felt menaced. That, coupled with the creepy feeling as the unseen ascending bubbles tickled his body, made him decide to give up the dive.

Two days later the area was put on alert as clouds of smoke were seen emerging from the sea nearby and the area experienced a 'seismic swarm' of earthquakes. That explained the dirty water. Nothing like a good shake to stir things up.

Now all is quiet again. Must have been a teenage tantrum.

# CRADLE
## TO
# GRAVE

**Below** *Bilum bags holding up to 40kg of pumpkins are being carried by these women.*

*Story and photographs by Keith Briggs*

Traditionally, Papua New Guineans have not used saddle or pack animals, or constructed wheeled vehicles to transport cargo. Apart from those who used canoes on the coast, rivers or inland waterways, people themselves have carried everything that had to be moved from one place to another. Heavy pots and large items for house building were carried on men's shoulders. Except for such big and awkward items, virtually everything was carried in bilums (string bags) by men, women and children.

About the only preparation made for an expected baby was the weaving of a new bilum. If it was completed in time, the baby would be made snug in a nest of soft leaves inside the bag, spending most of its first year or so in there, hanging down mother's back while she walked and worked. At the garden, baby's bilum was hung from the lower limb of a shady tree where it swung gently while mother was at work. On the homeward journey, mother would employ another bilum for the vegetables, fire wood, bamboo water

tubes filled at the creek and a piglet or two just to top up the load.

We have seen the bodies of people who have died at the medical centre, carefully folded before rigor mortis has set in, fitted into large bilums to be carried back to the village by grieving relatives. The bilum truly serves from the cradle to the grave, where often it is carefully laid with the deceased, holding personal possessions.

The picture has not changed much today except in urban areas.

Generally, women carry the heavier loads, and their bilums are suspended down the back from the wide net band around the forehead. Men generally wear theirs at the side, suspended from the opposite shoulder. The title page picture (p. 37) shows a lady with 40kg of pumpkins in her bilum, and her daughters carrying 30kg, 20kg, and 10kg respectively. They had walked on a rough jungle trail for one and a half hours bringing them in for sale.

Many roads that were pushed through PNG in the early days were built with hand labor, using spades and perhaps some wheelbarrows. Huge loads of stones for building up embankments or bridge buttresses were carried in these most versatile cargo movers. Today, as open truck-loads of people travel along established roads, virtually all of them carry bilums which hold their valuables and the results of trips to the trade store.

Colorful, expensive examples have become a part of women's attire, topping off their bright skirts, meri blouses and head cloths. These special bags are made by unravelling knitting wool and reworking it into a strong,

**Far left** *Rolling fibres into string.* **Centre** *'Tulip' tree bark provides the fibre.* **Below** *The bilum weaver dyes cords as she goes, using turmeric for yellow and bixa for red.* **Below right** *Deft fingers and keen eyes create the patterns.*

high tensile cord. Sometimes wool is blended with the traditional fibre to give the color of the former to the strength of the latter. There are some beautiful designs to be seen, including ornate patterns where the makers have worked their names, a greeting or a verse of scripture into the face of the bag.

Colored nylon 'bilum twine' is sold in stores, and although it saves hours of tiresome string making and is extremely strong, it does not have the suppleness of wool and traditional string and tends to fray good clothes as it rubs back and forth.

The tree, Gnetum gnemon L. or 'tulip' in pidgin, which has edible leaves and fruit, is the one that yields the raw material for traditional bilum making. The bark is stripped from the young saplings, the inner fibrous layer is peeled from it and hung to dry. Once dry, it is teased to give fine fibres that are rolled on the thigh to form two light threads. With a quick, deft motion of the heel of the hand, these two are twisted together to become one uniform cord. The loose ends of the two threads are left frayed to enable the

**Right** *Similar stitches from different weavers.*
**Below** *Bixa pod and turmeric root for dyeing.*

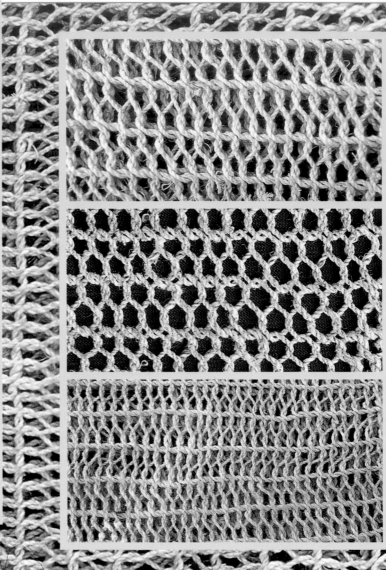

next lengths to be blended into them. Some women put a fine talc-like powdered clay on their skin to smooth the rolling operation.

Strips of pandanus leaves about 10mm wide are prepared, on which to form the stitches and regulate their size. A metre or two of cord is made at one time. For coloring the string, ripe pods from the Bixa Orellana L. bush are on hand. The pods are split revealing rows of large seeds which are coated with a red liquid dye that soaks into the cord as it is drawn through the half pod being squeezed on to the cord. It dries fairly quickly and can soon be worked into the bilum.

For the yellow row, the cord is drawn through a cut in the yellow ginger-like root of Curcuma Longa L. or turmeric, which imparts its rich ochre color. This too dries quickly enough to be worked into stitches along the pandanus leaves without delay.

The end of the prepared cord is threaded through the loop of the stitch to be formed and pulled through by winding the slack thread onto the thumb and little finger in a very quick back and forth flicking of the hand. Once through, the stitch is held from slipping by pressure from thumb and forefinger of the left hand. The bulk of the string is dropped from the 'loom', the end threaded through the next loop and the slack swiftly pulled through again as the thread is whipped around the fingers of the flicking hand. Apart from the time-consuming task of making the string and dyeing it, each stitch takes about 15 seconds to form. A medium sized bilum with open weave has around 4,000 stitches!

Introduced materials are fast replacing the traditional string, but modern technology has not yet replaced the traditional bilum makers still seen in many places in PNG today.

**Left** A bilum takes shape, a common village scene. **Below** Pandanus leaves are used as guides to ensure uniformity.

# Fish

Story and photographs by
Keith Graham

It was an opportunity not to be missed, to spend a week fishing for Papua New Guinea's legendary black and spot-tailed bass. We were about to embark on a fishing adventure, exploring virtually untouched rivers on the Gazelle Peninsula, East New Britain.

I had come to Rabaul with my fishing companion John Cross, and our floating home was a comfortable 12-metre boat fully equipped for extended chartering. Two aluminium dinghies, with electric and petrol outboards were safely stowed, provisions loaded and the engine fired up.

As we left Rabaul I put a trolling lure out the back. Within 100 metres the reel screamed off, followed by a 10-minute fight with a giant trevally of about 10 kg. Not a bad start. The inner and outer harbors of Rabaul have a variety of sportfish including sailfish, trevally, wahoo and barracuda, and the occasional blue marlin and yellowfin tuna in season.

As we rounded Cape Gazelle and headed south both rods arched as pick handle-sized wahoo took the lures. Leisurely we reeled them in then prepared them for dinner.

By dusk we had reached our overnight anchorage, with a freezer box half full of fish. We entered Runge, or as the locals prefer to call it, Putt Putt Harbor. We archored and our fresh fish feast was soon cooking; inquisitive villagers pulling alongside to pass the time of day.

Unable to resist the opportunity to wet a line I baited up with a strip of local baitfish called murumburr. Our host, Allan ('Jamo') Jameson, had assured me it was the most successful bait to use. Leaning the rod against the gunwales, I continued to enjoy the meal. Then the rod jumped into the air, the reel drag humming. When the fish surfaced it turned out to be a mangrove jack of around 2kg. Within the next two hours we caught 10 more jacks, the biggest 2.2kg.

Our destination next day was the Powell River which feeds Henry Reid Bay, a shallow inlet that drops off to more than 1500 metres depth within a kilometre of shore. Permission was sought from the nearby plantation owner and villagers before we ventured near the river mouth. Here all the fish belong to the nationals and as a matter of courtesy the correct approaches have to be made.

Formalities taken care of, we anchored in the river mouth, unloaded the dinghy and prepared to make our first sortie into this virgin territory. Magnum graphite baitcasting rods were complemented by heavy duty reels, loaded with 10kg breaking strain line. We knew only too well the tackle breaking capabilities of these bass. Lures were mainly handcrafted hardwood timber with stainless steel fittings and oversized heavy duty hooks.

Five kilometres upstream we noticed fast water movements on a deep log-covered bank. I made the first cast. Nothing. Next cast seemed unproductive, until I went to lift the lure out of the water. Just then about 5kg of bass tried to engulf the lure right at the boat. I tentatively cast back into the same area and this time he connected and led me upstream. I had the reel drag fully tightened up and this fish pulled line off as if there

# Tales

was no pressure at all. I locked my thumb on the spool and the fish began to turn. Then he decided that he did not want to play and took me straight into a sunken pile of debris. Exit one lure, and I was left with a burned thumb and aching arms.

Next time we tightened the reels drag with a pair of pliers and had the electric outboard ready to go flat out in reverse once the fish was hooked. Back to the same spot, I cast again, and a fish struck. I held the rod high and with the motor going in reverse, I gritted my teeth waiting for something to give. It worked and soon we netted our first bass of the trip, a 4kg spot-tail. This was exhilarating and

during the afternoon six more were caught.

But now came the real challenge — to find the elusive black bass which apparently fought twice as hard as its cousin the spot-tail. It took two days to work out the whereabouts of the black bass. In the process we took spot-tails on fly gear and found other species in this river system such as mangrove jack, trevally, bream, tarpon and jungle perch.

Near the saltwater inflow of the river mouth there was considerable current. I placed my lure in among a group of sunken logs when it suddenly stopped, as though caught on the timber. But timber doesn't pull and I

realised this was a fish of incredible strength. This virtual 'hand-to-hand' combat ended when I locked up the reel with my thumbs and to our elation a 6kg black bass popped to the surface. John cast straight back into the same area and hooked an equally good fish. Two black bass in five minutes was amazing! We had been told that only spot-tail inhabited this coastal region, so to find these prized sportfish was an added bonus to the trip. This was fishing at its very best.

We continued to enjoy bass fishing on the Powell and on other, smaller rivers in the area. In several rivers on our return leg we caught bass. The most

noteworthy was Warangoi River which is the closest major outflow to Rabaul. Here we managed to haul two black bass from their hide. They weighed 3kg and 5kg. Again the point was proved that black bass were plentiful in the Rabaul area, and no doubt will be fished for more often in the future.

On the scale of a kilo of fish per kilo of line breaking strain, in my opinion there is no fish that compares with the sheer power of the PNG black bass, closely followed by its cousin the spot-tailed bass. Both species are unique to New Guinea and are fast gaining a reputation among international sportsfishermen as 'the ultimate challenge'.

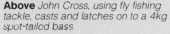
**Above** *John Cross, using fly fishing tackle, casts and latches on to a 4kg spot-tailed bass*

# TUMBUNA PAIA

Story and photographs
by Keith Briggs

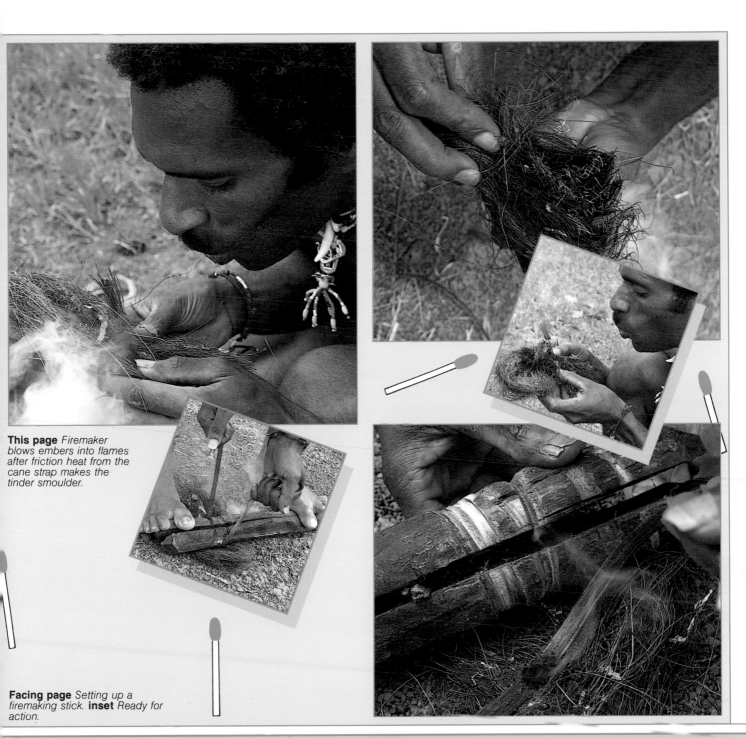

**This page** *Firemaker blows embers into flames after friction heat from the cane strap makes the tinder smoulder.*

**Facing page** *Setting up a firemaking stick.* **inset** *Ready for action.*

When the head flies off the match as we strike it along the side of its box, or if it fails to light we mutter about the poor quality of things these days. We tend to overlook the fact that a box of 40 or 50 matches is amazing value for a very few toea. It also helps balance our thinking to remember that until quite recently for many people the business of getting a fire going entailed a fair bit of time and a lot of skill.

Before the humble match found its way into the bilums (string bags) of people in the bush each man had to carry the equipment needed for making fire. Carefully wrapped in bark to keep it dry was a stick 2.5 to 5 centimetres in diameter, split half way along its length. A small twig wedged in the split held the two halves slightly apart. In the parcel too were pieces of tough, flexible cane and a ball of fine fluffy fibre resembling a bird's nest. This is obtained from under the smooth outer bark of the palm from which axe handles

are made. A similar product is made by rubbing and fraying the bark of other suitable trees.

A wad of this tinder is placed on the ground and the split stick laid on it. A piece of the cane is passed around the under side and the stick held firmly with both feet. Grasping an end of the cane in each hand the operator pulls it rapidly back and forth around the stick with a strong upward pressure. The high degree of friction thus produced powders the soft dry sap wood and the heat ignites it. At the

point of the split on the under side of the stick this smouldering powder drops in a concentrated spot on the tinder which the man quickly picks up and blows into a blaze.

A man can have healthy flames in half a minute or so. Even though matches are generally available, a lot of men in isolated places still carry their traditional fire lighting gear with them just in case.

So if we get a couple of duds in a box of matches we are still not doing too badly are we?

# Dominique Martin

Story and photographs
by Liz Thompson

**Above** *The artist, Dominique Martin,*
**right** *'Bilas' (finery), oil on canvas.*

Dominique Martin has
lived in Papua New
Guinea for nearly seven
years and during that
time has become very involved in the
promotion and the encouragement of
Papua New Guinean artists. Now
president of the Arts Council of Port
Moresby she continues to be
instrumental in the organisation of
Moresby's annual Arts and Crafts
Exhibition and continues to be
involved with the students working
their way through the National Arts
School where she taught part-time for
three years.

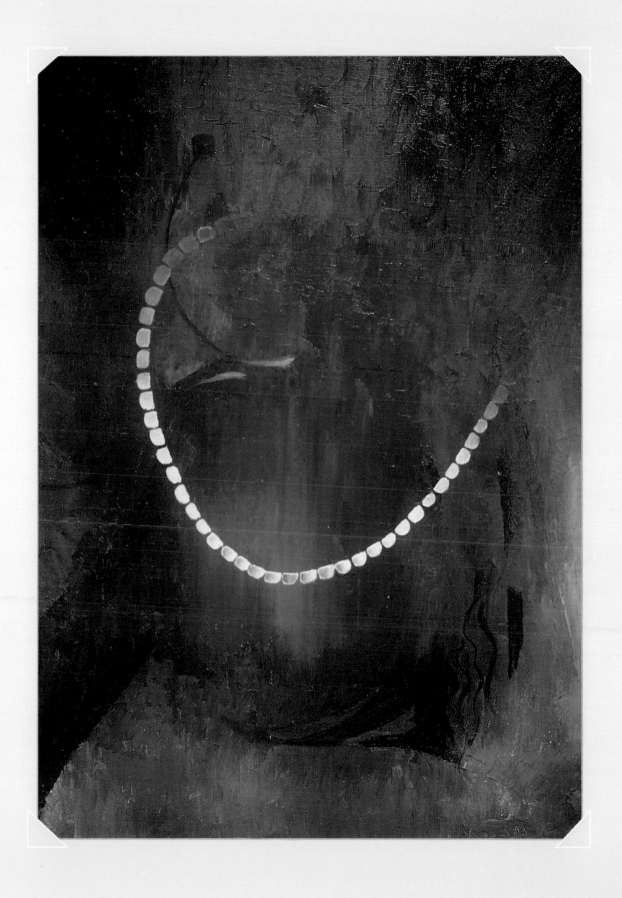

123

Facing page *Untitled oil rendition of bilas.* **this page, above** *Untitled watercolor of bilas.* **top right** *'Plumage' watercolor.* **right** *'Fish' watercolor.*

In addition to her deep involvement in the official structures surrounding contemporary arts in the country she is also a highly talented artist in her own right and is a prolific painter. Since arriving in PNG she has created consistently, inspired by her surroundings. In 1985 she exhibited her work at the Waigani Art Centre, in 1988 at the Lae Lodge and she regularly puts work into the Arts and Crafts Exhibition.

She is dedicated to improving the conditions for artists and raising the profile of contemporary arts in the country. One of the problems she points to in encouraging young artists is the complete lack of arts education in primary schools and the limited amount available up to grade 10.

"When students come to the National Arts School many of them have had no art education whatsoever," she said. "The exception are those who come from the National High School. Lecturers find it necessary to go out recruiting sometimes, touring the country, looking at students and trying to find people interested in developing their art education."

Originally from Paris, where she did a Diploma of Drawing and Visual Arts, she has travelled widely, living for five years in Tanzania and 18 months in Denmark. Her husband, an Australian, wanted to return to this side of the world but Australia did not appeal to Dominique. PNG did and that was where they decided to live. "The color was the thing that interested me most," she said. "When

**Above** *'Nellie' 1985 oil on canvas.* **top right** *'Untitled' oil.* **right** *'Ela Beach' 1984 oil on canvas.*

I started to travel around the country, to Woitape, the Port Moresby Show, Yule Island, suddenly I started to see all the exciting color, the dance and the life this country had to offer.

Brightly colored and often 'exotic', her work is, in some instances, almost Gauginesque.

"The people on the coast are the same as the people that Gaugin painted; the color and the light are the same as in Tahiti. I was from that kind of background, that was what I studied, so it's obvious my first

instinct was to paint like that."

Her painting has become more focused, more abstract as she has become more familiar with her surroundings and able to pick out the details of things she sees around her. Her work is wide ranging but among her most characteristic paintings are those of bilums, large and small in subtle washes of watercolor. Depicting the varying designs of traditional bilum bags made of rolled bark and colored, traditionally with local ochres, they are painted in watercolor washes.

Originally she painted with oils and started to use watercolors only after arriving in PNG. Oils were a problem. "Using oils here is disappointing because of the climate," she said. "You spend months and months working on a canvas and then, months later, it's covered in fungus. A watercolor dries much faster. I'm trying to get the same results out of them as I had been getting with oils."

The free-flowing, expressive paintings hardly hint at her formal training as an architect, though the

**Above** *Untitled market scene in oil.*

two interests, painting and architecture were, she says, in conflict. "Training in architecture has very directly affected my painting. I can't do both. I have to choose one or the other. Architecture is very stiff; it's creative in a very formal way, so it sort of stifles me. A lot of my work is geometrical and broken into geometrical areas and I think that's a direct influence from my training. But eventually I had to stop architecture in order to paint. I tried to do both for a while and my painting became really tight and my architecture and drawing became really loose."

Her work bears witness to her choice — easy, free flowing and a legacy to the color and vitality she obviously draws from her surrounding environment and the other artists she has contact with. As an expatriate artist, it seems PNG does for Dominique Martin what Tahiti did for Gaugin.

# Tree Kangaroo

Story and photographs by Jean-Paul Ferrero

**Above** Grizzled tree kangaroo, Torricelli Mountains.

Until last year, nobody in the world scientific community had heard about Scott's tree kangaroo. Not that the macropod bearing its name was unknown to the villagers of the Torricelli mountains in the Western Sepik region of Papua New Guinea but simply because the animal had neither a common name nor official status as a species described by zoology.

A substantial financial gift from the estate of a wealthy Sydney woman gave the kangaroo a name and Dr Tim Flannery, from the Australian Museum, the means to undertake a long term study of the 'Dendrolagus scottae'.

Most Australians would be surprised to learn that the rainforests of north Queensland shelter two species of kangaroos that climb trees. On the island of New Guinea, nearly everyone knows about the seven species under local names such as ugwa, d'bol, timboyok, ulea, wangoerie, yonquile and the now famous tenkile. All have been hunted as highly prized food by the people of PNG and Irian Jaya for eons.

The challenge of discovering a major species of mammals — a male tenkile weight is estimated at 20 kilograms — toward the end of the 20th Century is tantamount to finding another set of Great Pyramids.

**Left** Base camp in Wabute village. **above** Tim Flannery (left) and expedition members study maps of the search area.

Tim Flannery's quest started three years ago when, by accident, the claw of an unknown animal came to his attention during a field trip in the Torricellis. Back in Sydney, he realised it had to belong to an undescribed species of tree kangaroo. This was later confirmed when the body of a young tenkile killed by dogs was sent to the museum. The single most important clue to the identity and habitat of the new species came in the encounter between a live joey and Father Pat McGeevey in the village of Fatima. In 1989, the Irish, Peter O'Toole-lookalike priest was presented with a young animal orphaned by a hunting party. Tender care did not

**Below** *Tim Flannery examines a water rat among hunters' haul in the Torricelli Mountains.*

however prevent the youngster from dying before the wildlife authorities got to it.

In February, 1990, Tim Flannery, Roger Martin, a zoologist involved in the study of the Australian Bennett's tree kangaroo, a film crew and myself set off for the Torricellis in search of the tenkile.

In the village of Wabute, our base camp for the next two weeks, we met Lester Seri and his assistant, Viari, from the PNG Wildlife Department.

The forested slopes of Mount Somoro seemed to be within touching distance from our stilted house. We were soon to spend the better part of a full day climbing through thickly vegetated escarpments and crossing rivers to reach the summit of Mount Somoro, in the heart of the tenkile habitat.

Soon the local hunters disappeared in the mossy labyrinth of the upper montane forest. A very different hunt for them: We all definitely preferred a live tenkile to a dead one. With a lame dog and a pregnant one left behind, the chances of success were remote. No tenkile was sighted on the first night.

Besides this project, Tim is working on a comprehensive survey of the mammals of PNG. Days were spent processing the catch secured by our local helpers.

As a wildlife photographer, my interest grows with the size and any wealth of color displayed by my models. Tim's enthusiasm fires with rare specimens of drab appearance: "See this little guy," he said, handing me a trap in which a small-sized rat was caught. "That's only the fourth I have ever seen."

Taking it to my small tent, by then not only sleeping quarters but also portable field studio, I managed to get a few frames of the rare northern hydromine, unknown to me until now and most likely destined to future obscurity for the rest of the world.

I certainly got more excited when a yellow-spotted, tube-nosed bat had been caught in one of our mist nets. "Looks like a new species," declared Tim.

The following nights were no more successful for our hunting friends. The evening camp fire was now the venue for interviews and exchange of stories about the tenkile. It transpired that the older hunters had killed many kangaroos in earlier days. "Not so many these days," professed our cook, Anton. It was to be the most understated prophecy as we headed

**Left** Tropical rainforest of the Torricelli Mountains. **below** Undescribed species of frog found on Mount Somoro.

Left *Small-eared nyctophilus bat in the Torricelli Mountains.* **above** *Rare northern hydromine (water mouse).* **below** *Torricelli Mountains tropical rainforest.*

back toward the village after almost a week in the forest.

After a short flight from Lumi, we landed to the only access point to our second search area: the small airfield of Utai. We were to trek to the village of Fas No. 3 along the Gredike River flowing from an unnamed range at the eastern end of the Bewani mountains.

We were informed that no tenkile existed in the area but the 'fiwo' were plentiful up the mountain. The description fitted the tenkile physical attributes. We settled for a change of name.

In this desolate part of the country, people rely much more on hunting than their counterparts in more 'urbanised' areas. The Fas hunters had plenty of hungry looking dogs and exuded more confidence in their abilities than the Wabute villagers.

Next afternoon the commissioned hunting party walked into the village with three dark-furred tree kangaroos. The male had been killed but the female and young were alive. There was a sudden rush of activity: one grabbing a camera, one a tripod, sound recording equipment and instruments of measure in an effort to welcome the 'tenkile–fiwo' into the world of scientific recognition.

Upon examination, and to our greatest discomfort, Tim declared: "They are not tenkiles." Then he added: "I have never seen such tree kangaroos. They look like Doria's tree kangaroos but are much too small."

We did not return to Sydney empty handed. We had a couple of 'fiwo' specimens, now being subjected to DNA analysis to determine if they are a new species or a sub-species of the Dorias, and we had valuable information about the tenkile.

We now have a much better idea as to where the elusive kangaroo is waiting for our next expedition.

# KINA TREES

**Story and photographs by David Eastburn**

In April 1975, Papua New Guinea introduced its own currency in preparation for Independence. The kina replaced the Australian dollar and the toea, the cent.

The units of the new currency adopted the names of two important forms of traditional shell money. The toea is an armband cut from a large cone shell, usually the leopard cone which was used for trading along the coast of Papua. It is still used as part of some bride price payments, especially in the Central Province.

Kina is a pidgin and Kuanua word for the shell of the goldlip pearl oyster which was cut into crescent shape and used for both traditional 'money' and also personal decoration.

The kina was the most important traditional currency in the western half of the Highlands. Kinas were used for bride price, compensation payments and, most importantly, in complex ceremonial exchange systems. These exchange systems, called tee by the Enga, mok-ink by

the Mendi and moka by the people around Mt Hagen, involved the exchange of often thousands of kina shells for pigs, to gain status for the clans involved.

Kinas still are used in exchanges in the Highlands, but are not nearly as important as in the past. Today they compete with other forms of wealth, including paper and metal kina.

Before the arrival of Europeans, shells were not plentiful in the Highlands. Each shell had to be

traded from the coast through many hands. Only very important men possessed many. Recollections of older village people, and the written and photographic records of the first European visitors, reveal that cowrie shells were relatively common but kinas were rare and usually in poor condition. Even broken pieces of kina were scarce.

The Mendi people, from the South Highlands, mounted slivers of the rare kina shell on wooden crescents to create 'shomps'. It was hoped that the 'shomps', with the help of some magic, would attract complete shells. If a complete shell did eventually arrive, the original sliver was taken from the crescent and mounted with tree resin on the new shell and called a 'shell shomp'.

'Shomps' were very highly valued and were paraded on important public ceremonial occasions to show clan wealth. They began to drop out of circulation in the early 1930s, as more and more complete high quality kinas were traded from European sources. A few Mendi clans retain these rare heirlooms.

According to the gold prospecting Leahy brothers, the widespread belief in the western part of the Highlands when they arrived in 1933, was that kina shells grew on trees. Some of the first men contacted in the Upper Waghi were keen to accompany the Leahys back so they could obtain some kina tree cuttings for themselves. Their belief was supported by legend.

Legends often explained the origin of kina shells as fruit or bracket fungus which grew on magnificent glowing trees with beautiful red leaves. The groves of kina trees were owned by spirit beings who occasionally provided shells to favored humans. Within the groves sang the most beautiful birds.

Fallen leaves beneath the trees, on closer inspection, were revealed to be broken pieces of shell.

The legends frequently included a misunderstanding or the breaking of a taboo by the humans which resulted in the loss of access to the trees and their precious fruit. According to a Foi legend from Lake Kutubu, following the breaking of a taboo a landslide carried the shells into the Kikori River which washed them to the Papuan Gulf. From that time on, the Foi people received only a few kina shells which were slowly traded back from the coast.

An embellishment to this once common belief was told by Pumas of Karel, the first Mendi man to work with Europeans. Pumas returned to his village from Mt Hagen in the 1940s and brought kina shells, hard navy biscuits and a mirror. He is reputed to have told his people that he had been to the land of the dead where there were trees which bore kinas as their fruit. He went on to explain that the kinas grew in pairs and within each pair was enclosed a biscuit!

Shells, and especially kina shells, were the key to the relatively peaceful exploration of the Highlands by the Australians. Had they not been able to provide shells, which were so valued by the Highlanders, they would not have been nearly so welcome.

**Title page** *'Kina tree' of banknotes.* **far left and below** *Rare 'shomps'.* **top** *Kinas on display.* **right** *Foi woman with kina necklace and toea armshells.*

**Above** *Mendi ceremonial dress includes both kina and bailer shell decoration.*

entered the Highlands, including difficulty in buying food and numerous conflicts as the patrol passed through the Tari Basin and Mebi Valley, were largely a result of not having shell to trade. In his book, 'Papuan Wonderland', Hides wrote :

"All these people wanted pearl and cowrie shell, though I could see little of this among them. They held up little broken pieces of pearl shell, and with a questioning look, asked us if we had any. I had to tell them that we had not; but their quick searching eyes discovered the pearl buttons on our clothes, and before night had fallen we had no buttons left."

The following year, Ivan Champion and Bill Adamson led a patrol through the same region without incident because, after Hides' experience, they carried plenty of shells for trade.

James Taylor is reputed to have been the first to realise the value of shell as trade in the Highlands, after observing the way one Anga man examined a rope of money cowries. Shells were something the people of the interior of PNG valued. Shells, especially kinas, were to the Highlanders like gold to the prospecting Europeans. In February 1933, Taylor gave the Leahy brothers some shell for trade as they left Benebena on a prospecting expedition to Kainantu. He soon received requests for more!

The Highlanders eagerly accepted shells for food, building materials and labor. Cowries generally came from around Rabaul and kina shells at first came from Manus Island. As demand increased, kinas were obtained from the pearling centre of Thursday Island in Torres Strait.

The shells from Thursday Island arrived whole, in wooden cases. The Highlanders had to be shown how to cut, clean and polish them and soon began to prefer uncut shells to the finished crescent which was originally received.

In 1934, the Leahy brothers chartered aircraft to bring shells from Thursday Island to use as trade during their gold prospecting expeditions in the Highlands.

At first factory goods, such as beads, knives, axes and colored cloth, were carried on patrols as trade for food and labor. These were frequently rejected by the Highlanders who were confident about the quality of their own fine stone axes. Bamboo made excellent knives and their own decorations were more than equal to the beads and cloth offered by the Australians.

The choice of manufactured goods, which were acceptable as trade along the coast, proved almost fatal to the members of the Strickland-Purari Patrol in 1935. Poor relations with the villagers once they

People around Mt Hagen named the Leahys the 'Shellmen' as aircraft with cases of kinas began to arrive.

Missions became involved in the shell trade in 1934 to service their Highland stations. Children from mission schools along the coast collected shells for use in the Highlands.

Millions of shells (some say as many as 15 million) of all types were brought into the Highlands by the Australians between 1933 and 1963. In 1936, the Leahy brothers were flying in about 500 kinas per month to meet their food and labor bills. The famous Hagen-Sepik Patrol of 1938-39, the largest patrol in Papua New Guinea history, carried with it about 800 kilograms of shell for trade.

Shells, unlike manufactured goods, took a lot of organisation to obtain and were relatively expensive by the time they were flown into the Highlands, but they were 'natural' trade items. Not all types of shell were universally accepted. White egg cowries (Ovula ovum) were highly valued in the eastern part of the Highlands but were unacceptable in the west where they were replaced as the basic currency by kina shells.

Some of the older Highland men can recall their excitement when they first received shells from the Australians. They could not believe their good fortune and would just look at the beautiful objects for hours. They wrapped the shells carefully in leaves and stored them in their houses but could not resist unwrapping and admiring them at every opportunity.

Interest in shells in the Highlands was intense and men spent hours discussing the qualities of various shells and handling them with the enthusiasm of connoisseurs. In the eyes of the Mendi, the quality of a kina shell was determined by size, thickness, the condition of the outside 'skin', symmetrical shape, a reddish-gold color and 'light' which made it glow in the sunlight. The color was enhanced by polishing and rubbing the outside with red ochre. The mother-of-pearl surface inside the shell was not important in

assessing a shell, in fact it was deliberately not looked at in case the outside turned white as well.

Kina shells were carefully packed in multi-layered wallets of pine bark and pandanus leaves and bound with dozens of turns of string. The unwrapping of each shell at an exchange was a long, deliberate process. As each layer was slowly removed, the anticipation and excitement of onlookers heightened. The shells were then laid out in lines on beds of broad dark-green leaves to show up their reddened surfaces. After long discussion, they were graded according to quality. Considerable time was spent re-arranging the lines of kinas to reach the correct order.

In 1947, District Commissioner James Taylor introduced cash (pounds, shillings and pence) into the Highlands as payment for goods and services, along with shells. At first people rejected the cash because there were few trade stores in which to spend it. When stores became more common, kina shells were one of their most popular items for sale. In the 1970s, shells could still be purchased in some trade stores in the Southern Highlands.

Kina shells are losing their importance in exchanges in the Western and Southern Highlands and Enga Provinces. Today

banknotes, trucks and other valuables are displayed next to kina shells. The magic kina trees of Highland mythology have been replaced by man-made 'trees' displaying banknote leaves.

**Top** Discussing and assessing the attributes of kinas at a ceremonial exchange. **above** Anga man displays wealth in the form of cowrie shells, tree kangaroo's teeth and pig tusks.

Dead ahead are rocks, rapids and raging water. The adrenalin is rushing and the command "Hard forward" is barely audible above the raging current. "Harder," I scream as a boulder looms menacingly. We paddle furiously, pushing ourselves to the limit. Our raft bounces madly through the rapids then, with our last available strength, we drive its nose around the top end of the rock and, with a flick of the steering paddle, drop into a narrow chute and cross the pumping pressure waves.

We were four, intrepid adventurers from Pacific Expeditions: the first people to set foot or raft blade in this gorge. Floating through jungle on a raging river, buried deep in the heart of Papua New Guinea, this was the culmination of two years, planning, dreaming, poring over maps and aerial reconnaissance flights down the river gorge.

The Angabanga River starts as a thin trickle in the Papuan Highlands. It drains the southern face of the Owen Stanley Range, picking up speed and force as it drops. Where we "put in", at the entrance to the gorge, the river runs wide and fast.

Village people gather around to watch us prepare, talking to Charlie, our Papuan paddler. Their looks of interest change to disbelief as he explains our journey. Meanwhile we pump up the raft. As the length of flat yellow expands into a fully inflated raft their eyes widen in amazement, and their comments become more animated.

Casting off into the smooth, swift rapids and we leave villages and people behind as the river takes a twist. Following our route on the map, we see contour lines stacked up steeply around the bend, indicating a gorge. We decide to stop and scout. David takes the bowline in hand and leaps for the nearest rock. But the current is too strong and he lands in the river, coming up spluttering, soggy cricket hat hanging

The water races the canoes through steep ravines **below**. The canoeists are well prepared for their adventure **inset**.

# Rafting the Angabanga

**Story and photographs by Grant Trewenack**

over his ears, sunglasses awry at the end of his nose. I laugh uproariously but this is no time for frivolity as the boat careers around the bend, with David in tow. We drag him hastily on board.

In the gorge proper now, smooth, fast lines of water, rapids and rocks. We are feeling a little nervous. Around every corner is a new unseen set of rapids. We stop to scout where possible but sometimes there is no suitable "take out". We then have to run the rapid blind: read and run, paddle fast, stay alert, pulling the raft around and down those long glistening water chutes.

Further downstream appears the only section we must check out before we attempt it. Our earlier air reconnaissance had indicated a stretch full of large boulders. As we flew overhead the rocks had seemed so close packed that it appeared we'd have to walk and portage our gear across. Hard work.

We stop to scout and find a fast narrow channel which might take us through. We decide to try it as there is no alternative. A magnificent waterfall plummets from 60 metres overhead into a rock pool at our feet. Ordinarily we'd be gasping in awe but, preoccupied with the risks ahead, we barely notice it.

Pushing off and paddling strongly, we position ourselves for the run. It is a slalom course through a zigzag of rocks. We negotiate the first couple with ease, but the raft is screaming. We squeeze inside a rock, bounce and spin off the next, then pull ourselves into line for the drop into a narrow slot. Intent on holding our position, I am the last to see it: a boulder lies in front.

The river bowls over it carrying us with it and we drop into the jaws of a gaping, boiling cauldron of water. As the tail end of the raft drops out from under me, I flip over backwards into the regurgitating "hole". The raft hits, buckles and fills with water but its momentum carries it

through. As for me, I come up gasping, just in time to hear Dave advising the others, "Don't worry about him, he can swim". We pull into slack water to bail the boat and congratulate ourselves on surviving.

The Angabanga narrows and deepens but we are through the most exciting rapids. The water runs faster on the outside curves so we place ourselves into position for a smooth glide. For the first time we are free to appreciate the grandeur of our surroundings. "Gorgeous Gorge", we call it. The jungle is so thick it seems to grow into the river. The cliff walls are sheer; water cascades down from either side. Trees cling tenaciously on a spider's network of roots. Everything is bathed in the glow of the afternoon tropical sun. We have stepped out of time and paddled into the forgotten land.

A long sandy beach looks like a good place to spend the night. The backdrop for our campsite is something from a Rousseau painting. Two of the largest palm fronds I have seen form an umbrella over the fire. The jungle is a profusion of rainforest ferns, enormous palm trees and carnivorous plants. Underfoot is the mulch of a thousand years of rotting rainforest. We barbecue steaks, brew coffee and laugh at one another's slapstick antics; mostly we're aglow with the illusion that we have discovered this magnificent jungle site.

We are awake at sunrise and afloat before the sun has entered the gorge. We lay back, talk lazily and watch the jungle drift by. The cool morning hours are the best time to observe birds: a pair of Papuan hornbills swoop through the gorge, a brahminy kite spirals upwards on a draft of air, screeching sulphur-crested cockatoos and multi-hued lorikeets escort us downstream. Reptiles are everywhere: water dragons bask on rocks, overhead a green treesnake lies coiled endlessly on

itself. Charlie, with his local knowledge and trained eye, spots our first crocodile, 1.5 metres long. It sees us at the same time and flops lazily into the water. Its gnarled head surfaces, less than a metre from the boat, jaws agape, grinning at us. We stay there transfixed; I realise it has probably never seen men before, but this is no time for social exchange. Dave jabs it on the snout with his paddle and we make a fast getaway. Further downstream a piece of petrified wood suddenly comes alive: another crocodile. These freshwater crocs show no aggression and are content to watch this strange yellow object float down the river.

Mountains give way to plains and jungle gives way to kunai grass. After a couple of hours we see a clearing, young banana palms, and a small garden house. This is our first sign of civilization and an indication that we are nearing journey's end.

We're feeling elated by now. David laughs quietly to himself: "It's the river," he says, when asked. "It's so much better than I had ever hoped for."

We have discovered the perfect weekend jungle river run, through uninhabited, untouched rainfall wilderness, enough excitement for any enthusiast, yet relatively safe; beautiful wildlife and paradisal waterfalls.

Inquiries about Angabanga River rafting can be directed to Pacific Expeditions, PO Box 132, Port Moresby. Telephone 25-7803.

# POSSUMS

*Sugar Glider*

Story by Tim Flannery,
drawings by
Peter Schouten

Americans and Australians are familiar with possums, or opossums as they are sometimes called, for these animals form an important part of the fauna of both continents. But despite the familiarity of possums, few visitors to Papua New Guinea realise that this country is home to the most spectacular array of possums to be found anywhere on earth. Indeed, the closest that many visitors come to possums in PNG is the sight of a piece of bright fur in a head-dress, or a tail hanging from some young dancer's neck.

Papua New Guineans know their possums as either Kapul in Tok Pisin, or cuscus in English, and although they might sometimes be hard to find, from PNG's farthest flung islands to its highest mountain tops, there are possums to suit every occasion. The great diversity and beauty of the possums of Australia and PNG have prompted Peter Schouten and myself to produce a fully illustrated book on these creatures. The drawings in this article are only some of the 60 or so that will appear in the final work, which will also include information on almost everything that one would want to know about these charming creatures.

PNG is home to the very largest as well as some of the smallest of possums. The world's largest possum species is unique to PNG, and is very rare. Known as the black-spotted cuscus, it can weigh up to seven kilograms and be almost a metre and a half in total length. It is found only in the undisturbed lowland jungles of northern PNG, and although it was first found in 1906 by a German explorer it is so rare that it has remained virtually unknown until very recently. Its obscurity was not helped when the original, and for a long time the only known specimen, was destroyed by

Sugar Glider

*Coppery ringtail*

the bombing of Vienna during World War II.

Among the smaller of PNG's possums is the delightful sugar glider. This kitten-sized species (weighing about 100 grams) is widespread throughout most of Australia and PNG, including many offshore islands. Active by night, the sugar glider uses the membranes of skin between its fore and hind legs to glide from one tree to the next. By day, up to a half dozen animals snuggle together in a tree hollow. Usually there is only one dominant male and his 'harem'. Sugar gliders eat a diverse range of foods. There are reports from Australia of groups of them attacking birds as large as guinea fowl. However, their more usual foods include sap and nectar. Despite the cuteness of this species, some Papua New Guineans regard them with dread. It is a common belief among the Goilala people of Central Province, for example, that sorcerers can transform themselves into sugar gliders, and travel by night to spy upon their enemies. The curious clicking call that this species sometimes makes is thus a cause for apprehension if one is hunting alone at night.

Perhaps the most unusual of PNG's possums are the so-called skunk possums. There are four species of skunk possums, all of which occur in PNG, so these animals can be thought of as truly unique PNG treasures. Anyone familiar with North American skunks would, if confronted with one of these creatures, see that they share many similarities with real skunks. For like true skunks the skunk possums are patterned boldly with black and white stripes. These colors are a warning sign in nature, and remarkably they warn of the same danger in both species. For the skunk possums, like true skunks, have glands around their anus that produce an evil smelling fluid.

When walking through PNG forests many people comment upon the distinctive, musky scent that emanates from some trees. Few, however, realise that the smell is the result of a skunk possum having been in the vicinity.

Skunk possums also have an unusual choice of food. One often sees old decayed logs in the forest that have been chewed and pockmarked all over. These logs are the feeding sites of skunk possums. By night the possums visit them, and listening carefully, locate the huge grub-like beetle larvae that bore through the rotting wood. Once a possum hears the jaws of the grub munching through wood, it uses its powerful front teeth to expose the larva. Then it brings in to play a most unusual mechanism. One finger on each hand is longer and in some cases thinner than the rest. The possum uses it to fish for grubs. If the entire grub cannot be easily extracted by the teeth, the possum deftly inserts its long finger and extracts it whole.

A final possum that merits a mention is the so called coppery ringtail of the high mountain forests. Visitors lucky enough to witness a traditional marriage in the highlands, or even to be staying in a village when a hunter returns, are likely to see this species, for it is one of the commonest varieties. During traditional marriages live possums can form an important part of a bride price. The animals are located while they sleep by day in tree hollows, then brought out and either bound to poles or put in cages, and presented at the marriage ceremony. If you are lucky enough to witness such an event, check to see if the fur of the possums has a metallic lustre similar to burnished copper. If so, then the chances are that you are looking at a coppery ringtail.

*Spotted cuscus, male in foreground.*